Accidental Nuclear War

Thinkers' Lodge, Pugwash, Nova Scotia, which welcomed the first Pugwash Conference in 1957, and most recently welcomed participants to the July 1989 Workshop.

Photo, kindly lent by Anne Eaton, of drawing by an unknown artist.

Accidental Nuclear War

Proceedings of the Eighteenth
Pugwash Workshop on Nuclear Forces

Editors:

Derek Paul, Michael D. Intriligator and Paul Smoker

Canadian Papers in Peace Studies

1990 special issue

Science for Peace/ Samuel Stevens
Toronto
1990

Science for Peace
University College
University of Toronto
Toronto, Canada M5S 1A1

Samuel Stevens & Company
University of Toronto Press
5201 Dufferin Street
Downsview, Ontario
Canada M3H 5T6

Printed in Canada

Canadian Cataloguing in Publication Data

Pugwash Workshop on Nuclear Forces (18th : 1989 :
Pugwash, N.S.)
    Accidental nuclear war

(Canadian papers in peace studies ; 1990 special issue)
Includes bibliographical references.
ISBN 0-88866-634-9

1. Nuclear crisis control – Congresses. 2. Nuclear
crisis control – Psychological aspects – Congresses.
3. Nuclear arms control – Congresses. 4. Nuclear
warfare – Congresses. I. Paul, Derek.
II. Intriligator, Michael D. III. Smoker, Paul.
IV. Science for Peace (Association). V. Title.
VI. Series.

JX1974.8.P8 1989   355.02'17   C90-093876-5

Contents

Psychological Aspects

vi

Preface

This book is based on the July 1989 Pugwash Workshop on Accidental Nuclear War, which took place in Pugwash, Nova Scotia, in the setting of the first international Pugwash conference (1957). Science for Peace gratefully acknowledges the financial support of the the Pugwash Park Commission, without which this book would not have been produced.

Just as Cyrus and Anne Eaton hosted that first conference thirty two years ago, now Anne Eaton, with Gian Brenciaglia and his wife Sue, graciously hosted the 1989 Workshop.

This special issue of the Canadian Papers in Peace Studies departs from our past practice of publishing monographs by a single author — essays, as it were. The opportunity to bring out a new book on Accidental Nuclear War was irresistible. Though this book is the Proceedings of the July 1989 Pugwash Workshop, it is both more and less than that. The nature of the introductory chapters is such that we try to provide some background (chapter II) as well as to summarize the substantive points of the Workshop (chapter III). We go beyond the actual proceedings in that we draw, in both these chapters, on additional experience, knowledge, and insights of four of our authors. At the same time the discussion as such is not reproduced here — in fact it would be contrary to Pugwash tradition to ascribe particular points of informal discussion to the people who made them.

The paper by Intriligator and Brito is a revised version of an earlier paper presented at the December 1986 Pugwash Workshop on Accidental Nuclear War, held in Geneva. Though their paper was not available in its present form at the July 1989 Workshop, the recommendations it puts forward were presented and discussed, and many participants were familiar with the 1986 version of the paper. George and Gottfried were the rapporteurs of the July 1989 Workshop, and their original report has appeared in the Pugwash Newsletter vol. 27, number 1, July 1989. Their present paper is a slightly revised version of the Newsletter report.

The rest of this book consists of written papers submitted to the Workshop and discussed at the Workshop, plus one verbal presentation that was discussed and subsequently written up. Two papers submitted and not presented or discussed (because the authors were not present) have been omitted; but I think that the thrust of these papers, which were general overviews, is not lost in this book.

I express my thanks to Peigi Rockwell, who assisted without flagging in the preparation of the text; and to Geoff Rockwell, who advised and assisted in various essential linkages with the University of Toronto Computing services. Ruth Hayward generously volunteered to proofread the final text, for which we are most grateful.

** ** **

Books submitted to the Publications Committee of Science for Peace for this series are each considered on their merits, having due regard to the purposes of Science for Peace. In addition, the Committee seeks authors for books on topics that are thought to be of special importance at the time. The Committee has a general policy of submitting typescripts to independent referees for comment, but is not rigidly bound by this policy, and also seeks to avoid long delays when material of timely relevance is submitted.

Derek Paul, series editor
Physics Department
University of Toronto
Toronto,   M5S 1A7

Foreword

This book constitutes the Proceedings of a meeting held in Pugwash, Nova Scotia, 18-20 July 1989, which was the eighteenth in a series of Workshops on Nuclear Forces held in the framework of the Pugwash Conferences on Science and World Affairs. (For a brief description of Pugwash Conferences see page xiv). This particular series of Workshops was initiated in January 1980, that is, immediately after the NATO *double-track* decision of December 1979 that in the short run led to the deployment in Europe of new US nuclear-armed missiles — ground-launched cruise missiles and medium-range ballistic missiles (Pershing II) — but that was also instrumental in setting into motion the process that led to the total elimination of all US and Soviet ground-based missiles having ranges from 500 to 5500 km (Intermediate-Range Nuclear Forces Treaty, December 1987). The first Pugwash Workshop of this series also met in the immediate aftermath of the Soviet military intervention in Afghanistan, the termination of which is another positive, recent development. All these Workshops (except, precisely, the eighteenth) were held in Geneva, Switzerland, and their main purpose was to facilitate progress toward nuclear disarmament, acting to some extent as unofficial backgrounds and sounding boards for the official negotiations whose main visible threads were the Soviet-American talks (START) in Geneva. Hence the main topics, discussed in these Workshops by knowledgeable and influential experts, had to do with the composition of nuclear (and conventional) forces, nuclear (and conventional) strategy, the role, prospects and possible pitfalls of trying to develop strategic (possibly space-based) defences, and the foreseeable (and desirable) prospects of arms control and disarmament. The danger that nuclear war might somehow erupt — and cause catastrophic destruction — was, of course, always present in our minds, serving as a main motivation for dealing with these topics. We hoped that our discussions, involving experts from all sides (Americans, Soviets, Europeans from the NATO, WTO and neutral countries, and also some individuals from other parts of the world) would contribute to avert that danger.

As the international atmosphere improved, concrete progress in arms control and disarmament appeared imminent, while the prospect of a deliberate armed conflict engaging the main powers appeared instead more and more remote. It then appeared appropriate to focus on another concern, namely, that a nuclear war — or any use of nuclear weapons — might occur in an accidental, or unintended manner. Hence this question was identified as the theme for the fourteenth Pugwash Workshop of our series (Geneva, 13-14 December, 1986) and then again for the eighteenth Workshop (Pugwash, Nova Scotia, 18-20 July 1989). In both cases much attention was devoted to the psychological components of this question, involving the behaviour of individuals under stress and the screening of people dealing with nuclear matters; in addition, of course, to the command and control of nuclear weapons, the strategic postures, the nuclear arsenals, the channels of communication among decision-makers in nuclear-weapon countries — all factors relevant to the danger of accidental nuclear war. Accordingly, the participants in these meetings comprised individuals with a broad spectrum of competence, ranging from experts in psychology and psychiatry to experts on the command and control of nuclear weapons. Equally broad were their national-political-ideological backgrounds (see page 163 for the list of participants in the eighteenth Workshop). They all attended, following in the tradition of all meetings organized in the framework of the Pugwash Conferences on Science and World Affairs, in their personal capacities, and not as official representatives of government or of any institution. All the papers printed in this book were written on the same basis of personal knowledge and opinion.

A report on the *Fourteenth Workshop on Nuclear Forces: Accidental Nuclear War* is printed in the January 1987 *Pugwash Newsletter* (Volume 24, No. 3).

A report of the *Eighteenth Pugwash Workshop on Nuclear Forces: Accidental Nuclear War* is printed in the July 1989 *Pugwash Newsletter* (Volume 27, No. 1). The wealth of excellent papers that had been written for this Workshop, but could not be included in the *Pugwash Newsletter* for lack of space, suggested a separate publication; the more so since a book, published in this series (*Canadian Papers in Peace Studies*) provides an excellent opportunity to bring these papers to the attention of a wider readership.

After having explained the origin of this publication, it is a pleasant duty for me — in my capacity as Secretary-General of Pugwash — to thank the Publications Director of Science for Peace for having eagerly agreed to publish this book, the editors of this volume for their zest in volunteering for this task and in carrying it out, the two rapporteurs who have written a lucid and informative report on the Workshop (chapter III),

xii

and all those who took part in the meeting, in particular the authors of the papers appearing here; and, last but not least, all those who made possible the Workshop by providing the necessary financial and organizational support, in particular the Pugwash Park Commission, and the Carnegie Corporation of New York, as well as the many individuals in the village of Pugwash who volunteered their organizational help (especially Ray Szabo who coordinated these efforts), and our most gracious hosts, Anne Eaton, Giovanni Brenciaglia (Chairman of the Pugwash Park Commission) and his wife Susan.

Francesco Calogero

Secretary-General

Pugwash Conferences on Science and World Affairs

Pugwash Conferences on Science and World Affairs

The purpose of the Pugwash Conferences is to bring together, from around the world, influential scholars and public figures concerned with reducing the danger of armed conflict and seeking cooperative solutions for global problems. Meeting in private as individuals, rather than as representatives of governments or institutions, Pugwash participants exchange views and explore alternative approaches to arms control and tension reduction with a combination of candour, continuity, and flexibility seldom attained in official East-West and North-South discussions and negotiations. Yet, because of the stature of many of the Pugwash participants in their own countries (as, for example, science and arms-control advisers to governments, key figures in academies of science and universities, and former and future holders of high goverment office), insights from Pugwash discussions tend to penetrate quickly to the appropriate levels of official policy-making.

The Pugwash Conferences take their name from the location of the first meeting, which was held in 1957 in the village of Pugwash, Nova Scotia. The stimulus for that gathering was a *Manifesto* issued in 1955 by Bertrand Russell and Albert Einstein — and signed also by Max Born, Percy Bridgman, Leopold Infeld, Frederic Joliot-Curie, Herman Muller, Linus Pauling, Cecil Powell, Joseph Rotblat, and Hideki Yukawa — which called upon scientists of all political persuasions to assemble to discuss the threat posed to civilization by the advent of thermonuclear weapons. The 1957 meeting was attended by 22 eminent scientists (seven from the United States, three each from the Soviet Union and Japan, two each from the United Kingdom and Canada, and one each from Australia, Austria, China, France, and Poland).

From that beginning evolved both a continuing series of meetings at locations all over the world — with a growing number and diversity of participants — and a rather decentralized organizational structure to coordinate and finance this activity. By the end of 1988 there had been 158 Pugwash Conferences, Symposia, and Workshops, with a total attendance of some 7900. The Conferences, which are held annually, are attended by 125 to 250 people; the more frequent topical Workshops and Symposia typically involve 30 to 50 participants. A basic rule is that participation is always by individuals in their private capacity (not as representatives of government or organizations). International arrangements and communications are coordinated through small permanent offices in Geneva, London, and Rome, while National Pugwash Groups — usually sponsored and/or administered by academies of science — nominate participants from their countries and rotate the work of hosting meetings. Formal governance of the organization is by a 27-member Council elected at the *Quinquennial* Conferences held every five years since 1962; the President of Pugwash is the titular head of the organization; the Secretary-General has the overall executive responsibility.

The first half of Pugwash's three-decade history coincided with some of the most frigid years of the Cold War, marked by the Berlin Crisis, the Cuban Missile Crisis, the invasion of Czechoslovakia, and the Vietnam War. In this period of strained official relations and few unofficial channels, the forums and lines of communication provided by Pugwash played useful background roles in helping lay the groundwork for the Partial Test Ban Treaty of 1963, the Non-Proliferation Treaty of 1968, the Anti-Ballistic Missile Treaty of 1972, and the Biological Weapons Convention of 1972. Subsequent trends of generally improving East-West relations and the emergence of a much wider array of unofficial channels of communication have somewhat reduced Pugwash's visibility while providing alternate pathways to similar ends, but Pugwash meetings have continued through the seventies and eighties to play an important role in bringing together key analysts and policy advisers for sustained, in-depth discussions of the crucial arms-control issues of the day: European nuclear forces, chemical weaponry, space weapons, conventional force reductions, and crisis control in the Third World, among others.

Starting in January 1980, for example, Pugwash's series of Workshops on nuclear forces provided an off-the-record forum where not only military and civilian analysts but also some members of the official negotiating teams compared notes and sought solutions to obstacles in the official negotiations (18 Workshops of this series have been held until now, most of them in Geneva, Switzerland). The Pugwash chemical warfare Workshops — 14 of them since 1974 — have similarly engaged technical experts from the official negotiating teams, as well as academic and industry experts; this series led in early 1987 to the first visit of Western chemical weapons specialists to an Eastern European chemical-production complex, and Pugwash contacts were also instrumental in setting up the first access by a US expert to the medical records associated with the disputed 1979 anthrax outbreak in Sverdlovsk. The Pugwash study group on conventional forces, which originated in the European Security Working Group of the 1982 Pugwash Conference in Warsaw, has played a pioneering role in developing concepts for restructuring conventional forces and doctrines into modes less suited for attack, and in gaining credibility for these concepts with Eastern as well as Western military planners and policy makers.

While Pugwash findings reach the policy community most directly through the participation of members of that community in Pugwash meetings and through the personal contacts of other participants with policy makers, additional means of airing Pugwash ideas are also used. A quarterly Pugwash *Newsletter* — distributed worldwide to policy makers, past Pugwash participants, and libraries — contains communiqués issued by the Pugwash Council, summaries of issues addressed in Pugwash meetings and, with the authors' permission, excerpts from commissioned and proffered papers presented at the meetings. (The summaries are prepared by participant/rapporteurs and do not quote or commit other participants). The *Annals of Pugwash*, which have been published as a book series (now by Springer Verlag), contain the most significant communiqués, summaries, and papers from each year's activity. Participants are often interviewed by the press during and after the meetings, but in these instances they speak only for themselves and do not attribute statements made by others in the meetings (which are generally closed to the press, to foster uninhibited discussions).

Costs of operating the Pugwash offices in Geneva, London and Rome are met by a combination of donated services, contributions from individuals, from foundations, and from the National Pugwash Groups (in proportion to their participation and ability to pay: for instance, the US and Soviet annual contributions are equal at about US$ 25,000 per year). Cost of participants' food and lodging during meetings are generally covered by the host Pugwash Group; participants find their own support for travel costs, either individually or through their home Pugwash Groups. No honoraria or other fees are paid to participants in Pugwash meetings, nor to the officers of Pugwash (who serve on a voluntary — unremunerated — basis).

National Pugwash Groups in the West raise the funds they need from foundations and individuals, and in some instances from their governments (usually through national academies of science). In the socialist countries, costs incurred by the National Pugwash Groups are generally provided by the academies of science.

(November 1989)

I. Introduction

Derek Paul

The custodianship of nuclear weapons, and all that goes into preventing accidental explosions, or any other mishap that could lead accidentally to disaster, has been a profound military as well as civil concern since the first bombs were developed under military authority. To be the custodian of nuclear weapons is no small responsibility, and the only acceptable record for the discharge of that responsibility is the perfect record in which nothing went badly wrong. Previous generations of military officers generally did not have such demands for continuous perfection thrust upon them. It is something new in the life of the human race.

The success of the military organizations of the nuclear-weapon powers in handling their awesome responsibility without a single accidental nuclear explosion in over forty years has been impressive. It may even have given many people a false sense of security, enabling them to ignore the accidents that have occurred, some of which could more likely have led to accidental nuclear war than an accidental nuclear explosion, say, at a missile site. One can thus see that many have been lulled into the cozy feeling that nuclear war will not take place, since it is not likely to take place by deliberate action. Others, who are aware of the immense complexity of modern military organizations, of command and control, communications, and intelligence systems, of human fallibility, of the complex phenomena of crisis, and of unforeseen glitches in the best-designed technical systems, do not share that feeling of security. Serious accidents that have occurred did not result in accidental explosions or in war but did give rise to added international tension, or even crisis. Evidently we have been lucky. Time and time again, these other people say that the only way to make the world safe from nuclear war (including, emphatically, accidental nuclear war) is to dismantle the nuclear weapons. [1] This was said again at the July 1989 Pugwash Workshop, and nobody objected.

People who concern themselves with reducing the probability of accidental nuclear war are not necessarily those favouring major and rapid steps in bilateral or multilateral disarmament. They are those who, regardless of their political and disarmament stripes, have enough knowledge of part or of the whole complex situation to be aware of steps that might reduce the chances of accidental war, so long as the nuclear arsenals exist.

This book brings together as much background information as we could present in a small space, and as many recommendations as the participants could sort out in a two-and-a-half day workshop. Because the focus was on psychological, medical and other human factors as well as on the more usual political, strategic, and technical factors, this collection may prove valuable. Of course it is not complete — such accounts never are — but it is as comprehensive as we could make it.

Pugwash, which is an international organization comprising in all about 2500 scholars, ex-diplomats, retired senior military officers, and others, began its Workshops on Nuclear Forces at the time of the fast-dropping temperature in East-West relations late in 1979. For a few years thereafter these relations were so poor that an international crisis might have precipitated a war. There are indications in this book (chapter IX) that war may have been narrowly averted at least once in this period. The Pugwash Workshops, which were small and brought in people having directly relevant expertise, have been widely regarded as useful activities. In December 1986 Pugwash held its first such Workshop devoted to the prevention of Accidental Nuclear War, in Geneva. The report of that meeting is available in the *Pugwash Newsletter* Vol. 24, No. 3, pp. 72-86 (January 1987) [2]. Included (pp.77-9) is a paper by Lt-Gen. Lloyd R. Leavitt (US Air Force, Ret.), who at one time was Vice Commander-in-Chief, Strategic Air Command. Leavitt's paper, not reproduced here, is important because it delineates some scenarios that have been proposed as roads to accidental nuclear war, and which he claims can be ruled out; he gives the reasons. The

July 1989 Workshop, which he also attended, thus had the advantage of his valuable experience in these matters. I also believe the Workshop did not become entrapped in discussion of scenarios that could be thought to lead to accidental nuclear war, but are marginal in their credibility.

The July 1989 Workshop also had the advantage of some material from the 1986 conference on Accidental Nuclear War sponsored by Science for Peace [3]. The convenor of that conference, Michael Wallace, also participated in the July 1989 Workshop.

What we present here is not the end of the story. Accidental nuclear war will be possible, even if unlikely, as long as the weapons exist and can be activated. Nevertheless, some people favour continuing nuclear deterrence as a mode of existence offering the best route to security. Others feel nuclear deterrence is demonstrably not the appropriate mode of coexistence between nations or blocks of nations enjoying the level of mutual understanding and common interests that are held by NATO and the WTO, or by the USA and the USSR. But that is not the debate here. The arguments for making the world safer from accidental war do not depend on whether we believe in the appropriateness of current deterrence strategy. Such arguments must and do stand on their own.

Those who recommend specific steps for the reduction of the dangers of accidental war often tread a fine line. By assisting the military complexes to make their nuclear ploys safer, they may inadvertently help to prolong the deadly games. A good example may exist in the present pages. One of our recommendations is that US *PALs* technology be shared between the nuclear weapons powers. But if the trust needed to permit sharing of advanced military technology is already so well developed, should we not be making much more rapid strides toward abolishing the offending weapons multilaterally? Correcting faults and improving procedures — necessary and laudable steps — make it possible for well-meaning scientists to help to legitimate military activities that are at best questionable. So we return to the beginning. Nuclear war is not very likely to occur accidentally or

3

inadvertently in the near future. But it could happen. The sane and safe strategy is twofold: to pay proper attention to factors such as are discussed in this book, and to combine such efforts with a plan for the ultimate elimination of weapons of mass destruction.

The scenario of a world without dangerous war machines was beautifully outlined in the bilateral McCloy-Zorin agreement, signed by the USA and the Soviet Union in 1961. President Kennedy and Mr Khruschev were not held to ridicule because of it at the time, and there is no reason we should consider its objectives less valid now than then.

Postscript

In the few months since the July 1989 Workshop, there seem to have been several significant international events, bearing upon the future of peace and war. At the time of writing, 10 November 1989, the USA and USSR are about to introduce their first joint resolution in the UN General Assembly. East Germans are leaving the GDR unopposed, and a change of government there seems inevitable. It has just been announced that movement between East and West Berlin is again freely possible, after 28 years of the infamous Wall. In the West, conservative newspaper editors have even mentioned German reunification. Premature though such thoughts may be, the implications of changed governments in Poland, Hungary, and perhaps the GDR, will be enormous for the removal of nuclear weapons from Central Europe and, before long, the removal of foreign troops. Such trends will not occur without bringing new dangers. For stability under the new conditions, the entire meaning of NATO and WTO will need to change; whole classes of armaments will need to be eliminated and more defensive doctrines, strategies and tactics will need to be followed (see Afheldt, chapter VI). However, there will be resistance to such changes. Already, NATO is trying to establish itself in North America and has succeeded in persuading the Canadian Government to establish a first Canadian NATO base in Goose Bay. That is only the beginning. Frustrated in Europe, the militarists can look, at present with impunity, to the Arctic and to the Pacific. The dangers of accidental nuclear war are therefore not about to disappear completely in the space of a year or two.

Notes

[1] Regrettably, this call to disarm is often misinterpreted to mean remove the nuclear weapons regardless of what other armaments are left in place. Of course, this could be folly; the wiser nuclear disarmament advocates are fully aware of the inherent weakness of conventional deterrence, especially having regard to the nature of modern forces. Nuclear disarmament should be accompanied by, or preceded by a transformation of basic military philosophy and strategy in the direction of defensive defence (see Afheldt, chapter VI).

[2] The address of the Pugwash London office is: Flat A, 63A Great Russell Street, London, WC1B 3BJ

[3] The papers presented at the Science for Peace 1986 conference on Accidental Nuclear War were published in **Peace Research Reviews** Vol. X, Nos 3 and 4. An excellent report of the conference was produced by the Canadian International Institute for Peace and Security (CIIPS): Andrea Demchuck, **The Risk of Accidental Nuclear War**, CIIPS Report No. 3, 38 pp. The Conference Report is now out of print, but is still available from Science for Peace, University College, Toronto, Ontario, M5S 1A1.

II. Accidental Nuclear War: An Important Issue for Arms Control*

Michael D. Intriligator and Dagobert L. Brito

Introduction

What are the chances of an accidental nuclear war? At one extreme, popular writers and some journalists have tended to sensationalize this problem, exaggerating the chances of an accidental nuclear war in novels, films, and media accounts, going so far as to suggest that it is a virtual certainty [1]. At the other extreme, military and political leaders and some defense scientists have tended to minimize this problem, dismissing the chances of an accidental nuclear war in public pronouncements and symposia, going so far as to insist that it is, in effect, impossible [2]. Our view is that the chances of an accidental nuclear war lie between these two extremes, in that there is a positive probability of an accidental nuclear war but that it is neither "high" nor, over time, a certainty. Thus it is an issue that should be addressed in a serious way rather than being ignored either as a certainty or as an impossibility. In this paper we identify several different types of accidents that could lead to a nuclear war; we argue that there probably has been an increase in the probability of an accidental nuclear war in recent years **relative** to that of a deliberate nuclear war; and we suggest an agenda of several arms control initiatives, which could be implemented on a bilateral, unilateral, or multilateral basis, that could reduce the chance of accidental nuclear war.

Types of Accidents that Could Lead to Accidental Nuclear War

We interpret *accidental nuclear war* as any nuclear war without a deliberate and properly informed decision to use nuclear weapons on the part of the national command authorities of the nuclear weapons states. The nuclear weapons states include not only the major powers of the

6

United States and the Soviet Union, but also the smaller nuclear powers of the United Kingdom, France, and China [3]. Accidental nuclear war, as we are interpreting it here, is also called *unintended* or *inadvertent* nuclear war. While we consider the chance of an accidental nuclear war to be *small*, we will argue in Section 3 that it has, for various reasons, risen relative to the chance of a deliberate nuclear war and may have risen absolutely as well. It undoubtedly rises rapidly in a crisis situation, particularly in the presence of an announced or a de facto launch-on-warning or launch-under-attack policy, in which strategic weapons, particularly land-based ICBMs, are launched upon a confirmed warning of an enemy launch or a confirmation of an enemy attack.

Here we will identify different types of accidents which could lead to an accidental nuclear war, particularly in a crisis situation. We also provide some historical examples of each type, and we will use these types of accidents in the later two sections to illustrate the changing relative probabilities of accidental versus deliberate nuclear war and to develop an arms control agenda to reduce the chance of accidental nuclear war.

The initiating accident, which could result in an accidental nuclear war, could occur in any part of the warning and decision system, starting with warning systems, continuing through communications links at the level of the national command authority, and again continuing through communications links to field commanders. It could also occur in weapons carriers, in the weapons themselves, in delegated or predelegated authority, or in third parties. Some important cases include:

a) **Accidents in Warning Systems**

Warning systems, involving sensors detecting an enemy attack, must cope with two possible types of error. The first, a Type I error, is the failure to detect an actual enemy attack, due, for example, to system malfunction or the destruction of its weak links by the enemy, as in a decapitation strike that destroys the national command authority. The second, a Type II error, is the false signal of an enemy attack when there is, in fact, no such attack. Any warning system must determine

7

an appropriate tradeoff between these two types of error [4]. For example, a highly sensitive system might reduce Type I error but at the cost of a possible Type II error. Conversely, a highly selective system may minimize the chance of a Type II error but at the cost of a possible Type I error. Fear of a Type I error, of not acting when one should, could drive up the chance of such a Type II error, of acting when one shouldn't. An ideal system which reduces both types of error may be impossible to build or prohibitively expensive.

Since further action, including a possible retaliatory attack or launch-on- warning/launch-under-attack, is typically based on the warning systems signalling an enemy attack, the most important accidents in warning systems in terms of a possible accidental nuclear war are those involving a Type II error, with a false signal of an enemy attack [5]. If such a mistake were made in a crisis, particularly with false confirmation by backup systems, there is the possibility that weapons would be launched in the mistaken belief that an enemy attack were underway. Even without a launch-on-warning/launch-under-attack doctrine there could be false information of the destruction of ones own cities or missiles, which could lead to a strike meant to be retaliatory in nature, but, in fact, a first strike.

Historically, there have been numerous reports of false warnings in the US due to various causes, including atmospheric disturbances, a meteorite shower, a flight of wild geese, and a computer chip failure. In recognition of the possibility of such a Type II error a procedure is used in US warning systems (and probably also in other such systems) called *dual phenomenology,* requiring that any warning must be confirmed by a second independent sensor system using a different physical technique for observation. This procedure is extremely valuable in reducing the chance of Type II error.

An example of an accident with a warning system was the June 1980 incident at the North American Aerospace Defense Command (NORAD) in Cheyenne Mountain near Colorado Springs, Colorado. NORAD operators believed that a massive Soviet attack was in progress for some six minutes before they discovered that a training tape had been accidentally mounted on the computers and read as an actual attack underway. This Type II error represented a very serious accident, but did not lead to an accidental nuclear war largely due to the dual phenomenology procedure, since there was no confirmation from an independent system. But if the computer tape had been read into two different systems there then would have been (false) confirmation of a Soviet attack underway. If this had happened during a crisis and/or with a launch-on-warning procedure in use, it could have led to an alert and possibly even to a launch.

Another example of an accident involving a warning system also occurred in June 1980 at NORAD. A NORAD computer sent an alert signal to SAC that two Soviet submarines had launched ballistic missiles which were on their way to the US. Later signals indicated a massive launch of Soviet ICBMs. About 100 bombers and the Presidential airborne command center were readied for takeoff before it was discovered that this false alarm was caused by a faulty computer chip.

A third example of an accident with a warning system was the July 1988 attack by the US ship Vincennes on an Iranian civilian airliner in the Gulf in the false belief that it was an attacking warplane. One possible factor in this Type II error was the earlier Type I error in the Gulf, when the US ship Stark failed to attack Iraqi warplanes that were about to strike it. Sensitivity on the part of the Vincennes captain and crew to the earlier Type I error of not responding to an actual attack and the desire to avoid repeating such an error may have directly or indirectly led to the Type II error of taking action in response to a false signal of an enemy attack.

Yet another type of a possible accident involving warning systems would be training exercises, which could be accidentally interpreted via the warning system of the other side as an actual attack. For example, there are reports that US intelligence becomes increasingly nervous during Soviet Strategic Rocket Forces nuclear training exercises [6]. Similarly, Soviet intelligence became nervous during the NATO nuclear weapons exercise Able Archer in November 1983, with Soviet overseas agents alerted by the KGB.

b) Accidents in C^3I Systems

Another type of accident involves C^3I systems of command, control, communication, and intelligence. For a nation planning a deliberate attack such systems form the link between the national command authority and the operational units that would conduct an attack or a retaliatory strike. For a nation intending solely to retaliate against an enemy first strike, which is the avowed positions of both major nuclear powers, the C^3I system is the link from the warning system to the national command authority and then from the national command authority to the operational units responsible for a retaliatory strike. In either case accidents in C^3I systems could lead to a launch [7]. Accidents in such systems are particularly serious during a crisis situation or during high-level alerts when taking the *next step* may involve one's own launch or may trigger the other side to launch. They are also particularly serious when decisions are automated in a launch-on-warning system.

Historical examples of such accidents include various possible accidents with computers, misread or misinterpreted signals, and losses of electrical power. Such accidents, which have probably occurred in all national C^3I systems, but which have not been reported, have not led to accidental nuclear war because of redundancies in the system, because of requirements of confirmation by independent systems (comparable to the dual phenomenology requirement for warning systems), and because they, fortunately, have not occurred in crisis or high-level alert situations.

c) Accidents with Actual or Potential Nuclear Weapons Carriers

This type of accident involves the operational units responsible for launching nuclear weapons, and it includes a variety of possible carriers, including planes, ships, submarines, and missiles. Again, this type of accident is particularly serious during a crisis. For example, the probably accidental intrusion into Soviet airspace of the KAL007 airliner in September 1983 led to its destruction, likely because it was mistakenly identified by the Soviets as a

US military aircraft. This incident may thus have been the result of two accidents: the first by the Korean Airlines pilot in entering Soviet airspace and the second by the Soviet air defense system in wrongly identifying the plane as a military aircraft. If, however, it had occurred in a crisis the intrusion of an airliner into Soviet airspace could have triggered a major Soviet response, such as an increase in alert levels involving bombers in the air, missile-carrying submarines, and land-based missile systems on alert. This, in turn, could have triggered a US response, escalating the situation.

The October 1986 explosion and fire on a Soviet Yankee-class submarine in the Atlantic is another example of an accident with an actual or potential weapons carrier. The submarine, which later sank, was carrying nuclear weapons. Another such example is the April 1989 sinking of a Soviet submarine off Norway. These accidents could have, especially in a crisis, triggered a response, either because the US national command authority believed the Soviets were unsuccessfully attempting to launch their submarine-launched ballistic missiles or because the Soviets believed the US was responsible for the explosion and fire. In fact, they did not result in such a reaction partly because they did not occur in a crisis and partly because the Soviets notified the US of these accidents, in keeping with the 1971 Accidents Measures Agreement. This bilateral agreement of unlimited duration between the US and the USSR calls for immediate notification in the event of an unauthorized, accidental, or other unexplained incident involving a possible detonation of a nuclear weapon which could create a risk of the possible outbreak of nuclear war.

d) Accidents with Nuclear Weapons

Continuing down the chain from warning systems to C^3I systems to weapons carriers, the next type of possible accident could occur in the nuclear weapons themselves, such as accidental launches or firings of warheads.

As one historical illustration of such an accident, there was an explosion and fire of propellant fuel in a Titan silo near Little Rock, Arkansas in September 1980 following an accident in which a workman dropped a wrench down the silo. The nuclear warhead was not armed and could not explode, but there was a danger that the missile could have been launched by accident. In fact, the missile did launch, but it was destroyed on impact with the cover of the silo, which was not pulled back. If there had been an actual launch, however, even with an unarmed warhead, especially in a time of crisis, it could have triggered a Soviet response.

Another example of a potential accident with weapons is the enormous stockpile of Nazi munitions discovered in 1961 deep in central Russia which took months to remove. Had these weapons exploded by accident before they were discovered to be of Nazi origin the accident could have triggered a Soviet response in the mistaken belief that it was a strike on them, possibly from the US or possibly from another nation. A more recent example is the July 1984 explosion at a Soviet naval base on the Kola peninsula which, according to press reports, was so powerful that it was thought at first to have been a nuclear accident. Again it could potentially have triggered a Soviet response in the mistaken belief that it was a strike on them. Yet another example is the US cruise missile accident in West Germany in 1985. If it had resulted in an inadvertent launch it could have triggered a Soviet response.

One very useful feature on many nuclear weapons is the presence of Permissive Action Links (PALs), electronic locks that prevent the weapon from being armed without the explicit and specific instruction of the national command authority. Such PALs are present on all US nuclear weapons other than naval weapons, including submarine-launched ballistic missiles (SLBMs). Similar devices are thought to be installed on nuclear weapons of the Soviet Union and of other nuclear powers as well.

e) Accidents with Predelegated Authority

Predelegated authority involves the authority of field commanders to launch weapons at their own discretion in certain situations. With such predelegated authority the possibilities of accidents increase quite dramatically. For example, accidents in communication links with submarine commanders could, in a crisis, lead to accidental launch decisions in view of the lack of PALs on SLBMs. Similarly, early release of tactical nuclear weapons to battlefield commanders in time of crisis could lead to accidental use of such weapons.

f) Accidents involving Third Parties

Another category of accidents involves third parties, including the other overt nuclear nations of the United Kingdom, France, and China; possible covert nuclear nations such as Israel, India, Pakistan, and perhaps others; and national or subnational terrorist groups. An accidental or intentional launch by such third parties could, particularly in a crisis, lead to an accidental nuclear war.

The Changing Relative Probabilities of Deliberate vs. Accidental Nuclear War

Deliberate nuclear war involves the deliberate and informed decision and action of the national command authority, which could take the form of a retaliatory attack, preemption in anticipation of an attack by an actual or potential enemy, escalation from a local or regional conflict, or a premeditated attack. The situations described in the previous section, by contrast, involve various routes to nuclear war without such deliberate and informed decision and action, that is, an accidental nuclear war.

Deliberate nuclear war was justifiably the principal concern of the national command authorities and thus also of both their defense and arms control communities up to the late 1960s and early 1970s. Until that time there were either no or relatively few invulnerable weapons that could be used to deter the other side via a retaliatory second strike. Perhaps the greatest danger of a deliberate nuclear war was in the late 1950s and early 1960s, culminating in the Quemoy-Matsu crisis of 1958, the Berlin crises, and, most important of all, the Cuban missile crisis of October 1962. The Cuban missile crisis was, in fact, probably the closest the world has come to nuclear war. President Kennedy was quoted by Robert Kennedy as estimating the probability at that time of nuclear war as one in three.

Since the early 1960s there has probably been a reduction in the chance of deliberate nuclear war due to the effects of deterrence, especially mutual deterrence via the threat of a retaliatory second strike. Deployments in the 1960s and 1970s of invulnerable weapons, including hardened silos for land-based missiles and, especially, the deployment of submarine-launched ballistic missiles on nuclear powered submarines plus very large increases in the stockpiles of land-based and submarine-based ballistic missiles substantially reduced the chance of deliberate nuclear war through their mutual deterrent effect. Deterrence is a psychological-political-technical reality which has worked to reduce the chance of a deliberate decision to use nuclear weapons. If both major nuclear powers (and also the smaller nuclear powers) see nuclear war as suicidal, then they will avoid using nuclear weapons in virtually any situation other than as retaliatory weapons. The presence of nuclear weapons therefore plays an important role in deterring their use by other nuclear powers. This situation of mutual deterrence has existed since the early 1970s, making the world considerably safer against a deliberate nuclear war than in the earlier period. Thus, it is not just fortuitous that there have been no crises comparable to the Cuban missile crisis in recent years. While improved accuracies of current generation weapons have virtually diminished the potential retaliatory role of fixed-site land-based missiles, the recent development of mobile missiles and the potential deployment of concealable and mobile cruise missiles has preserved a triad of retaliatory capabilities — on mobile or concealed land-based ballistic or cruise missiles, submarines on patrol, and bombers on alert (land-based missiles in fixed and known sites are like submarines in port or bombers on the ground, constituting targets which are likely to be destroyed on a first strike).

Arms controllers are perhaps spending too much of their time and effort trying to deal with a previous problem, namely deliberate nuclear war, as in numerous studies of the Cuban missile crisis. This is a problem that has been largely solved via mutual deterrence, as achieved through the types and quantities of weapons now deployed. To some extent, the chance of accidental nuclear war probably has also been reduced due to the deployment of secure second-strike weapons, since warnings need not lead immediately to a crisis situation and there is less need for predelegation to field commanders. There are, however, several significant factors pointing in the opposite direction, leading to an **increase** in the chance of accidental nuclear war. There is, first, the growing complexity of the systems that protect and control nuclear weapons, involving many components, any of which could fail. In particular, the difficulty of communicating with submarines compounds the difficulty inherent in complexity, as do accidents involving mobile weapons carriers, including surface ships and rail- or road-mobile carriers. A second factor in the growing danger of accidental nuclear war is the greater automation and technological sophistication and the resulting shorter decision times over the last ten years for strategic warning and command and control systems, which are potentially susceptible to false alarms, computer failure, and human error. In fact, stopping a disaster may have become impossible due to shorter warning times, greater use of computers and accelerated communications, and the potential interactions between the C^3I systems of opposing nations, which could possibly lead to cascading instability. A third factor is the possibility of a launch-on-warning system, either in place or a de facto one which is in place during a crisis or alert situation. This may, in fact, be the most important factor. In such a system vulnerable land-based missiles are launched on the warning of an enemy attack to avoid their being destroyed on the first strike, the rationale being *use them or lose them.*

Thus, while the chance of a deliberate nuclear war has probably fallen due to recognition on both sides of their mutual deterrence relationship and the enormous possible losses in a nuclear war, the chance of an accidental nuclear war has, at the same time, probably risen due to the nature of newer weapons systems; the complexity, speed, and automatic nature of their command and control systems; and the possibility of an actual or de facto launch-on-warning system. For all these reasons, while the chance of an accidental nuclear war is probably still *small*, it has probably risen relative to the chance of deliberate nuclear war, especially during a political or military crisis. This change has not been reflected, however, in the arms control process, which still emphasizes deliberate nuclear war and which tends to ignore or to minimize the importance of accidental nuclear war.

A point to be emphasized is that accidental nuclear war is a **systems** problem more than a numbers problem. The chance of an accident depends more on the nature of the complex command and control system, including associated people, procedures, and equipment, than on simply the number of weapons. It is not necessarily the case, for example, that the chance of accident increases directly with additional numbers of weapons or, conversely, that reducing numbers of weapons can reduce the chances of an accident. Rather, it depends on how the weapons are configured, deployed, and commanded. Indeed, the development of a triad of retaliatory weapons, the deployment of large stockpiles of weapons, and the reduction in the vulnerability of weapons have probably **reduced** the chance of accident by reducing the chance of warnings leading to higher levels of alert or to crises, by restricting the extent of predelegation to field commanders, and by avoiding launch-on-warning systems for vulnerable weapons. The most serious accidents involving nuclear weapons, in fact, have relatively little to do with the numbers of such weapons and thus would not be mitigated by reduced numbers of weapons. Rather, they depend on four critical relationships in a very complex system involving people, who are subject to stress and fatigue; procedures, in situations not experienced before; and equipment, subject to failure or overload.

First is the relationship between the warning system sensors and the sensor system operators which can lead to potential accidents in warning systems. Second is the relationship between the sensor system operators and the national command authority, and between the national command authority and weapons operators, leading to potential accidents in C^3I systems and potential accidents with predelegated authority. Third is the relationship between weapons systems operators and the weapons themselves, which could lead to accidents with actual or potential weapons carriers and to accidents with weapons. Fourth is the relationship between nuclear nations and national or subnational terrorist groups, leading to potential accidents involving third parties. All of these are **system** problems, in which the number of weapons is, if anything, a secondary consideration. This is both important and valuable since it means that it is possible to reduce the chance of accidental nuclear war in various ways without simply reducing the numbers of weapons unilaterally and thereby possibly undermining or eroding mutual deterrence. In general it is necessary to balance the positive effect of nuclear weapons in establishing a mutual deterrence regime and the negative effect of nuclear weapons in leading to the possibility of an accidental nuclear war [8].

When considering the various critical relationships and the specific types of accidents possible, it is clear that accidents have already happened and that they will continue to happen. It is impossible to design a system completely free of the potential for accident, and the larger and the more complex the system the greater the potential for accident, particularly at critical and possibly highly fragile person-person or person-machine interfaces. The Chernobyl nuclear power reactor accident of April 1986 is instructive in this regard [9]. There were safety systems that probably would have worked, but that were turned off in order to conduct a test, comparable to a test or an alert involving nuclear weapons. A factor contributing to the cause of the accident (which involved a design fault in the control rods) was the occurrence of various operator errors, due, in part, to fatigue as they had to wait ten hours to conduct the test due to added unexpected power requirements downline. This case highlights the importance of operators as critical elements in a complex system. Another case illustrating the fragility of sensitive interfaces is the Bhopal accident in India.

Another instructive example is the Challenger space shuttle accident of January 1986, which involved a failure of a technical component. The calculated probability of such a failure before the accident was later found to be significantly lower than it should have been due to a variety of biases, much as military and defense experts tend to downplay the chance of an accident with nuclear weapons. Human factors also entered into this accident, in that indications from earlier launches of such a potential technical failure were not followed up; the two NASA officials responsible for such an inquiry over a year before the accident were transferred and neither they nor their successors pursued the inquiry.

Accidents can and do happen, and they can happen at any time. The chances of an accident leading to an accidental nuclear war increases significantly, however, in a time of crisis or in a period of international tension. In a crisis, weapons systems may be on an alert status; the national command authorities, field commanders, and sensor operators may all be under stress; there may be delegation of authority to launch weapons; and there may be a possibility of a launch-on-warning system put in place. All of these factors, both individually and by collective mutual reinforcement, significantly increase the chance of an accidental nuclear war. The chance of such a war cannot, however, be solved simply by added technological safeguards, which only add to the complexity of the system and thereby may **increase** the chance of accidents.

The next section presents some arms control initiatives that could reduce the chance of accidental nuclear war, especially in a crisis. These initiatives are presented in order to bring the arms control agenda up to date. The Cuban missile crisis, with a significant chance of a deliberate nuclear war, occurred over 25 years ago. Since then, the world has changed considerably, particularly with the advent of a mutual deterrence relationship and the presence of additional nuclear powers. Thus the arms control agenda should be augmented in such a way as to focus on the new realities. The increase in the chance of accidental nuclear war relative to that of deliberate nuclear war should lead to a corresponding change in the arms control agenda.

Arms Control Initiatives to
Reduce the Chance of Accidental Nuclear War

If *arms control* means, as it should, initiatives that reduce the chance of nuclear war, not simply limitations on or reductions in numbers of weapons, then reducing the chance of accidental nuclear war should be a significant part of the arms control agenda [10]. However, accidental nuclear war has **not** been an important component of the arms control agenda, which has tended to stress weapons limitations or eliminations.

This section proposes several arms control initiatives that could be adopted in order to reduce the chance of accidental nuclear war at various levels -- bilateral, multilateral, and unilateral.

Bilateral initiatives, involving the United States and the Soviet Union, might appropriately build upon the 1971 Accidents Measures Agreement. This agreement is still in force and, as noted earlier, the Soviet Union was in full compliance with it in notifying the United States about the explosion and fire aboard its submarine carrying nuclear weapons in the Atlantic in October 1986, in contrast with its delay in notifying other nations about the Chernobyl accident in April of the same year. The agreement calls for the immediate notification of the other party of any accidents and other unexplained incidents involving a potential detonation of a nuclear weapon which could create the risk of a possible nuclear war. The agreement should be strengthened to require notification both of accidents involving third parties and of threats involving nuclear weapons from other nations or from subnational groups, such as terrorist groups. Furthermore there should be agreements, in advance of the event, on to how to deal with these situations, possibly as part of the recently established crisis control centers [11]. The important initiative is **not** the creation of the crisis control centers, but that of designing procedures for notification, confirmation, individual or joint action, or other measures to deal with accidents, threats, crises, etc., which may or may not involve a new organization such as a crisis control center.

19

Given the short times involved in warnings, flights of weapons, and consequent decision times, it is important to decide **in advance of the event** how to deal with a wide variety of possible contingencies involving accidents, crises, and threats. Essentially a manual must be developed jointly and accepted by both sides, on procedures to follow in each of many possible contingencies that could culminate in nuclear war by accident.

A second bilateral initiative would be improved communications links between the United States and the Soviet Union via not only the additional upgrading and hardening of the Hot Line (already agreed to) but also via other independent means of communication such as existing commercial lines, existing military C^3I systems, and diplomatic communications via embassies — which can too easily be overlooked. Such improved communications would facilitate the implementation of notification regarding accidents and of agreements to deal with accidents and other contingencies.

A third bilateral initiative would be an undertaking or agreement to reduce reliance on and eventually to eliminate both vulnerable nuclear weapons, particularly fixed-site land-based ballistic missiles (the US Minuteman III and MX and the Soviet SS-18 and SS-19), and systems with short flight times. Such moves would reduce the incentives to develop a launch-on-warning system and reduce the chance of accidental nuclear war involving such a system. Bilateral agreements could also involve the elimination of accident-prone weapons systems.

A fourth bilateral initiative would involve an agreement or understanding to include a command/destruct capability for all missiles. Such a capability currently exists in the US for non-military missiles of NASA, but it does not exist for military missiles, other than for tests. Such a capability would be valuable in allowing accidentally launched missiles to be destroyed. Military commanders have resisted the introduction of such a capability, mainly because of the fear that it could be activated by an enemy. But such a capability could be protected by its coding or encryption. In fact, it would be similar to Permissive Action Links (PALs), the electronic locks which must be activated by the national command authority in order to arm nuclear warheads. Such locks can, with a high degree of confidence, be protected against interference. Similarly, the missile carrying the warhead should have the capability of being destroyed after launch if the launch were made in error, with this capability protected against interference. Such a capability apparently does not currently exist, meaning that even one accidentally launched missile could not be destroyed and thus might cause many deaths and could initiate a major nuclear exchange and even possibly a nuclear war.

A fifth bilateral initiative would be an agreement not to deploy antisatellite (ASAT) systems. Such systems could provide a stimulus to the deployment of a launch-on-warning system, which could trigger countermeasures leading to a chance of accident. Furthermore, the ASAT systems themselves could lead to accidents.

A sixth bilateral initiative would be an understanding or agreement to strengthen nonproliferation by building on the Nonproliferation Treaty and other agreements and institutions of the nonproliferation regime. Areas requiring further strengthening to prevent an accident that could result in nuclear warfare include: the limitation of nuclear exports by new second-tier nuclear supplier states; enhancement of safeguards against diversion of nuclear materials to states or terrorist groups; and bilateral understandings as to procedures to deal with any of the current overt or covert nuclear weapons states should one of them fall into the hands of irrational or irresponsible leaders.

While the above six potential bilateral arms control initiatives would be valuable in reducing the chance of accidental nuclear war, they should be enhanced to include multilateral extensions with not only the other nuclear weapons states but other states as well.

First would be an extension of the (strengthened) Accidents Measures Agreement to all nuclear weapons states and perhaps even covert- or near-nuclear states, involving immediate notification of all states involved concerning any accidents involving nuclear weapons (and also nuclear facilities) and agreements in advance on how to deal with various possible accidents or nuclear threats to prevent them from precipitating a nuclear war. Similarly, the current bilateral Agreement on the Prevention of Nuclear War, in force since June 1973, which calls for immediate urgent consultations if there is the risk of a nuclear conflict, should be extended to include all nuclear weapons states.

Second would be an extension of the Hot Line via an upgrading of all bilateral communications links among the nuclear weapons states, including possibly covert nuclear weapons states. Furthermore, there might be a multilateral agreement under which each nuclear weapons state agrees not to interfere with the national C^3I system of any other nuclear weapons state.

Third would be a multilateral agreement on limiting and eventually eliminating vulnerable nuclear weapons and systems with short-flight times. Fourth would be a multilateral agreement on incorporating a command/destruct capability in any missile armed with nuclear warheads. Fifth would be a multilateral agreement not to deploy ASAT systems so as to avoid their instabilities and vulnerability. Sixth would be multilateral strengthening of the existing multilateral nonproliferation regime to deal with new nuclear supplier states, to prevent diversion of nuclear material, and to deal with potential irrational leaders of nuclear weapons states.

In addition to these six multilateral agenda items, which build on comparable bilateral initiatives, there are some additional multilateral items which could reduce the chance of accidental nuclear war.

A seventh multilateral initiative would be an agreement calling for prenotification of any major military exercises and of missile flight tests and the exchange of observers, building on the existing multilateral agreement in Europe that was the product of the Stockholm Conference on Disarmament in Europe. This agreement can and should be extended to Asia and other regions and also to naval exercises.

An eighth multilateral initiative would be an agreement to share Permissive Action Links technology, command-destruct technology, and other such technologies in order to control nuclear weapons and to destroy accidentally-fired missiles. These technologies would be valuable for all nuclear (and near-nuclear) states to have in order to control nuclear weapons and to avoid an accident, even one in a non-central region that could widen into a global nuclear war.

A ninth multilateral initiative would be the establishment of an international early-warning monitoring system, possibly via the UN that would ultimately be independent of any national monitoring system but which would provide information as needed. (A proposal limited to monitoring by satellite, along these lines, was made at the 1976 Pugwash Conference in Mühlhausen and later by French President Valerie Giscard d'Estaing at the First UN Special Session on Disarmament in 1978) [12]. This initiative would be analogous, on a world-wide basis, to the US monitoring of possible troop movements in the Sinai between Egypt and Israel, which has promoted stability in this region.

Arms control initiatives can be **unilateral** as well as bilateral or multilateral. Some unilateral initiatives are counterparts of the bilateral or multilateral initiatives, but others are strictly independent in nature.

A first unilateral initiative involves actions to contain or deescalate potential crises. An example is the Soviet grounding of all military aircraft following the November 22, 1963 assassination of President Kennedy in order to signal that they would not be taking advantage of the situation.

A second unilateral initiative involves improvements in C^3I to ensure control and to avoid false commands or communications, including defenses, both active and passive, of such systems to ensure their survivability and reliability. Such steps would reduce the danger of a decapitation strike and eliminate the need for a launch-on-warning system.

A third unilateral initiative involves tight initial screening and frequent rescreening of personnel involved in nuclear forces and in C^3I for potential alcohol, drug, or psychological problems.

23

A fourth unilateral initiative, which is the unilateral counterpart of a bilateral (or multilateral) initiative, would be the elimination of weapons systems that are vulnerable or involve short flight times and thus might be perceived by a potential opponent as first-strike systems. For example, fixed-site land-based ballistic missiles might be unilaterally replaced by mobile or concealable ballistic or cruise missiles [13]. Such a replacement on either side would avoid encouraging a first strike by the other, signal that it is not planning a first strike, avoid the need for a launch-on-warning system, reduce the seriousness and time urgency of a crisis situation, and reinforce deterrence by strengthening second-strike retaliatory capabilities.

Finally, a fifth unilateral initiative would be defenses, both active and passive, of national command authorities, of C^3I systems, and of retaliatory capabilities to ensure their survivability and their reliability even in case of a crisis, an accident, or preemption. All nuclear powers need this capacity to retaliate in order to have the stability of a mutual deterrence relationship, which would considerably defuse the dangers of a crisis, reduce the danger of a decapitation strike by an enemy, and limit or eliminate calls for a potentially dangerous launch-on-warning system. The presence for each nuclear power of at least four *other* nuclear nations, each with protected retaliatory capability, would promote stability through deterrence and reduce risks of accident as each nuclear power has an incentive to prevent accidents and not to take risks.

Conclusion

Just as war may be too important to leave to the generals (and admirals), arms control may be too important to leave to the politicians and negotiators. They have continued to make use of the *old* approach to arms control, entailing an orientation which focuses on deliberately initiated nuclear war, an agenda which concentrates on weapons limitations or reductions, and a procedure which relies primarily on bilateral negotiations. A new approach requires rethinking in all three respects. First, the orientation should shift from deliberately initiated nuclear war to accidental nuclear war, as the relative probabilities have shifted, with a greater emphasis on accidental nuclear war relative to that of deliberate nuclear war. Second, the agenda should shift away from weapons limitations or reductions, which do not address the problem of accidents and which may themselves, if carried too far, be counterproductive, eroding mutual deterrence. Instead the agenda should treat **system** changes that would reduce the chance of a crisis, reduce the chance of an accident, reduce the incentive to develop potentially unstable launch-on-warning systems, and reduce reliance on short flight time or vulnerable weapons. Arms control should focus on reductions in the **chance of the use** of weapons whether deliberate or accidental, not just on reducing **numbers** of weapons Finally, third, the procedure should allow for multilateral as well as bilateral initiatives, recognizing the existence and importance of cooperation among all nuclear weapons states in treating a shared problem. Unilateral initiatives are very much to be encouraged, recognizing that they can be extremely important, that self-interest may be sufficient as a motivating factor, and that such approaches avoid some of the problems of negotiation, delay, and compromise inherent in bilateral and multilateral approaches to arms control.

We have proposed a series of initiatives to reduce the danger of a potential accidental nuclear war, involving a series of bilateral, multilateral, and unilateral initiatives. If any one were adopted it could be beneficial in reducing the chance of accidental nuclear war, but if several or all were adopted they would have a mutually reinforcing effect. We believe that they constitute a valuable new agenda for reducing the chance of accidental nuclear war, an important issue for arms control.

Notes

* This paper was originally developed for presentation to the Pugwash Workshop on "Nuclear Forces: Accidental Nuclear War," held in Geneva, December 13-14, 1986. We are indebted to the Workshop participants for their suggestions on it, especially Paul Bracken, Colonel-

General N.F. Chervov, Bernard T. Feld, Richard L. Garwin, John P. Holdren, Lieutenant General Lloyd R. Leavitt, George Rathjens, Jack Ruina, General H. A. J. Sturge and James A. Thompson, none of whom necessarily agree with the analysis and policy implications presented here. We are also indebted for further suggestions to Roman Kolkowicz, William Potter, and Bennett Ramberg at CISA; Robert Nurick at Rand, Ian Percival at Queen Mary College; and Mikhail Milstein at the Institute of the USA and Canada. An earlier version of this paper was published in **Current Research on Peace and Violence**, Vol. 11, No. 1-2, 1988, pp. 14-23 (a special issue on the threat of accidental nuclear war.)

[1] Of course there is a bias on the part of these writers and journalists — to sell their products.

[2] Of course there is a bias on the part of these political/military leaders and scientists — to reduce anxiety and to defend the systems they have designed or built. Understating the chances of accidental nuclear war by leaders and scientists is probably similar to the understating of the calculated probability of an accident on the space shuttle that was discovered in the course of the investigation of the Challenger accident, based on a compounding of various downward biases, combined with wishful thinking, suspension of critical assessments, etc. Similar biases appear in the calculation of the probability of accidents in nuclear power plants. It may take a serious accident involving nuclear weapons, as was the case with the shuttle, to convince leaders and scientists of the importance of this problem. There is, however, evidence that the problem of accidental nuclear war is recently being taken more seriously by policymakers, as indicated by establishment of Risk Reduction Centers in Washington, DC and Moscow.

[3] There may be other states with covert nuclear weapons or the capability of producing such weapons on relatively short notice, such as Israel, India, Pakistan, and perhaps others. They should also be included.

[4] The concepts of Type I error and Type II error are standard ones in statistical decision theory, Type I

referring to rejecting a true hypothesis and Type II referring to accepting a false hypothesis.

[5] See Bracken (1983), Britten (1983), and Frei (1983).

[6] Soviet strategic rockets have had training launches from operational sites. By contrast, in the case of US land-based ICBMs few training launches have taken place from operational sites, with almost all such training launches conducted from Vandenberg Air Force Base in California.

[7] See Goldwater and Hart (1980), Dumas (1980), Bracken (1983), Britten (1983), Cull et al (1983), Frei (1983), Blair (1985), Ford (1985, 1986), and Wallace et al (1986). For a Soviet perspective see Milstein (1986).

[8] The problem of the ideal size and composition of the stockpile of nuclear weapons can be considered a type of inventory problem. As in inventory theory it is necessary to take account of both **stockout costs** (involving a loss of deterrence to one or both parties) and **holding costs** (involving the chance of accidents potentially leading to accidental nuclear war).

[9] See Ramberg (1986/1987). For assessments of the earlier Three Mile Island accident see Kemeny (1979) and Flynn and Chalmers (1980). On psychological factors in accidents see Dumas (1980), Perrow (1984), Thompson (1985), and Solomon and Marston, eds. (1986). See Intriligator and Brito (1988) for an overview of nuclear war issues, including accidental nuclear war, which can be studied in terms of psychological factors.

[10] On arms control as reducing the chance of nuclear war see Intriligator and Brito (1987). See also Intriligator and Brito (1984, 1985).

[11] Simply establishing nuclear Risk Reduction Centers, as was agreed to by the US and the Soviet Union in May 1987, solves little and could even be counterproductive if, as a result of their establishment, political and military leaders believe that they have solved the problem of crises or accidents. The point is not that such centers be established but that their role and function be clarified and that there is some assurance that they would, in fact, be used in a crisis. On crisis management and risk

reduction/crisis control centers see Lewis and Blacker, eds. (1983), Roderick and Magnusson, eds. (1983), Blechman, ed. (1985), Ury (1985), and Blechman and Krepon (1986).

[12] See Dorn (1987)

References

Blechman, B., ed. **Preventing Nuclear War: A Realistic Approach** (Bloomington: Indiana University Press, 1985)

Blechman, B. and M. Krepon **Nuclear Risk Reduction Centers** (Washington, D.C.: Center for Strategic and International Studies, 1986)

Blair, B. G. **Strategic Command and Control: Redefining the Nuclear Threat** (Washington, D.C.: The Brookings Institution, 1985)

Bracken, P. **The Command and Control of Nuclear Forces** (New Haven: Yale University Press, 1983)

Britten, S. **The Invisible Event: An Assessment of the Risk of Accidental or Unauthorized Detonation of Nuclear Weapons and of War by Miscalculation** (London: Menard Press, 1983)

Broad, W. J. "Computers and the US Military Don't Mix," **Science**, 14 March 1980, pp. 1183-1187

Cull, C., A. Erskine, U. Hang, A. Roper-Hall, and J. Thompson "Human Fallibility in the Control of Nuclear Weapons," in S. Farrow and A. Chown, eds. **The Human Cost of Nuclear War** (Cardiff: Titan Press, 1983)

Dorn, W.H., "Peace-Keeping Satellites," **Peace Research Reviews**, X, nos. 5, 6, 1987

Dumas, L. "Human Fallibility and Weapons," **Bulletin of the Atomic Scientists**, (1980) pp. 15-20

Ford, D. **The Button: The Pentagon's Strategic Command and Control System** (New York: Simon & Schuster, 1985

Ford, D. "The Nuclear Time Bomb," **Peace Research Review**, May, 1986

Frei, D. **Risks of Unintentional Nuclear War**, (London: Croom-Helm, 1983)

Flynn, C. B. and J. A. Chalmers **The Social and Economic Effects of the Accident at Three Mile Island:**

Findings to Date (Washington, D.C.: US Government Printing Office, 1980)

Goldwater, B. and G. Hart "Report on Recent False Alerts from the Nation's Missile Attack System," **Report to the Committee on Armed Services, United States Senate**, (Washington, D.C.: US Government Printing Office, 1980

Intriligator, M. D. "A Better Alternative for START," **Bulletin of Peace Proposals,** (1989) 20:225-227

Intriligator, M. D. and D. L. Brito "Can Arms Races Lead to the Outbreak of War?" **Journal of Conflict Resolution** (1984) 28:63-84

Intriligator, M. D. and D. L. Brito "Non-Armageddon Solutions to the Arms Race," **Arms Control** (1985) 6:41-57

Intriligator, M. D. and D. L. Brito **Arms Control: Problems and Prospects**, Research Paper No. 2 (Institute on Global Conflict and Cooperation, San Diego: University of California, San Diego, 1987)

Intriligator, M. D. and D. L. Brito "The Potential Contribution of Psychology to Nuclear War Issues," **American Psychologist,** (1988) 43:318-321

Kemeny, J. **The Need for Change: The Legacy of TMI**, Report of the President's Commission on the Accident at Three Mile Island (Washington, D.C.: US Government Printing Office, 1979)

Lewis, J. and C. Blacker, eds. "Next Steps in the Creation of an Accidental Nuclear War Prevention Center," (Stanford: Center for International Security and Arms Control, 1983

Milstein, M. A. "On the Threat of an Accidental Outbreak of Nuclear War," (in Russian), **SSHA: Ekonomika, Politika, Ideologiya** (1986) 10:3-13

Perrow, C. **Normal Accidents: Living With High-Risk Systems** (New York: Basic Books, 1984)

Ramberg, B. "Lessons of Chernobyl," **Foreign Affairs,** Winter 1986/1987, pp. 304-328

Roderick, H. and U. Magnusson, eds. **Avoiding Inadvertent War: Crisis Management**, (Austin: The University of Texas at Austin, Lyndon B. Johnson School of Public Affairs, 1983)

29

Solomon, F. and R. Q. Marston, eds. **The Medical Implications of Nuclear War** (Washington, D.C.: The National Academy Press, 1986)

Thompson, J. **Psychological Aspects of Nuclear War** (Chichester: Wiley, 1985)

Ury, W. **Beyond the Hot Line: How Crisis Control Can Prevent Nuclear War** (Boston: Houghton Mifflin, 1985)

Wallace, M. D., B. L. Crissey, and C. I. Sennott "Accidental Nuclear War: A Risk Assessment," **Journal of Peace Research** (1986) 23:9-27

III. Workshop Summary and Discussion

Alexander L. George and Kurt Gottfried

The following account draws upon and attempts to reflect the Workshop discussions and material in working papers prepared by participants. The accuracy of this report is the responsibility of the rapporteurs alone; it has not been reviewed by other participants and would not necessarily be fully endorsed by them. Given the range of issues covered in the workshop and the richness of the papers and discussion, the rapporteurs have found it necessary to prepare a longer, more detailed report than is customary for Pugwash workshops.

Accidental and Inadvertent War: Definitions and Scenarios

Members of the conference were not able to agree on precise definitions of *accidental war* and *inadvertent war* [1]. Indeed, some questioned whether there is a meaningful distinction. On the other hand, and more importantly, there was substantial agreement on *scenarios* that could possibly result in an unintended and unwanted nuclear war and on a variety of *factors* that could possibly contribute to such wars. This report therefore uses scenarios to define the context of the discussion.

Accidental war received much more attention in the conference than inadvertent war. Accidental war can be defined as one that occurs as a result of a wholly erroneous or significant misinterpretation of tactical warning that the opponent has launched a substantial nuclear strike which leads, in turn, to *prompt launch* of major nuclear retaliation, where the term prompt launch includes both *launch-on-warning* of an attack that is underway and *launch-under-attack* [2]. Included in this definition is the possibility that what is in fact a small nuclear attack is misjudged in early attack assessment to be a substantial one.

Inadvertent war differs in that it is not tied, as is accidental war, to misinterpretations of tactical warning or to erroneously inflated early attack assessment. For example, according to one scenario, inadvertent nuclear war occurs because one side decides to *preempt* deliberately on the basis of its *erroneous strategic* warning that the opponent has decided to attack, and is making what appear to be *unambiguous* preparations to launch a major nuclear strike in the very near future but has not yet set his attack into motion [3]. ** (Strictly speaking, by definition, *preemption* is undertaken on the basis solely of strategic warning *without waiting for tactical warning* that the opponent's attack is already underway. In practice, of course, a preemptive war can be initiated on the basis of a combination of strategic warning and some partial but inconclusive tactical warning indicators or on the basis of a mixture of equivocal strategic and tactical warning.) A broader set of scenarios that culminate in inadvertent war, and which involve the decision-making context, will be considered in the later section entitled Inadvertent War.

Much of the conference discussion focused on factors (technical and human) that can contribute to different accidental and inadvertent war scenarios. Such factors can combine in different ways to cause war — that is, there are different paths that can lead to accidental or inadvertent war.

** *Editor's Note: Many people will think of this example as one of preemptive or deliberate nuclear war, since the attack is launched without sufficient evidence that an attack by the opponent was inevitable. Nevertheless, we have been convinced by the authors that there are terrifying and plausible scenarios in which the Hot Line would be ineffective or unavailable and the decision would have to be made on the basis of strategic and tactical information or misinformation. Scenarios of this kind are touched upon in Afheldt's paper, chapter VI, who calls it incidental nuclear war, because the likelihood of it happening is built into the structure of the broad military policy and strategy.*

For each of the technical factors we add a brief discussion of some of the preventive or prophylactic measures that were suggested by conference participants. Following that, we discuss some of the human factors that could contribute to either type of war: the impact of crisis-induced stress, organic illness, cognitive dynamics, disturbed emotional states, and sleep deprivation. Finally, since crisis is a major context in which accidental or inadvertent war might occur, we offer some observations about the importance and modalities of crisis avoidance and crisis management, and call attention also to the importance of the state of the overall US-Soviet political relationship as a factor affecting the prevention of nuclear war.

The Workshop identified a number of preventive measures that require and deserve additional analytical assessment and consideration by policy makers.

Accidental War

Crudely put, accidental war can occur as a result of an action (or actions) that triggers a nuclear attack not properly authorized by the National Command Authority (NCA) or by a legitimately predelegated command. One such trigger will be considered here: accidental (and/or unauthorized) launch of strategic nuclear weapons. In addition, accidental war may occur as a result of a systemic failure of the warning and command system.

Accidents at Low Alert Status

Should an accidental launch [4] occur when both sides are in a peacetime posture, or at a low alert status [5], most participants believed that the likelihood of serious consequences is minimal. It is not obvious that this confidence is justified, however, for the following reasons.

First, it appears unlikely that a breach of the complex safeguards (at least in the US strategic command system) could occur only at the level of a single silo or even one Launch Control Center. Therefore, an appreciable number of ICBM's might be fired in the event, to which low probability is attached, of an accidental launch. Second, by the same token, accidental launch from a ballistic missile submarine might involve more than one missile, and perhaps even the full complement. Third, as most strategic missiles are MIRVed, such an accident could involve casualties that dwarf human experience. Hence, even if an accidental launch did not trigger a launch-on-warning or launch-under-attack response (the two are referred to in this report as prompt launch since the distinction between them is not clear-cut) — the absence of such a response to accidental launch may be quite likely in peacetime since it might then have a high threshold — it is unjustified to ignore the possibility that such an accidental launch would lead to demands for revenge, exceedingly tense international relations, the fall of governments, and so forth, which could lead to a war that might begin at the conventional level and then escalate.

Innovations that could reduce these risks can be unilateral or cooperative.

Unilateral Measures

1. Command-Destruct Capability (CDC) on Strategic Missiles [6]

CDC permits the missile's owner to order destruction by radio command after launch (as in test firings). The US military is strongly opposed to CDC because it fears espionage that could compromise the ability to retaliate. On the other hand, if the National Command Authority could disengage CDC at the time it decides to launch so that enemy radio signals could not destroy a missile that had been launched on proper authorization, these objections seem to fall away [7]. CDC therefore appears to be a very promising technical means for reducing the accidental launch danger.

2. Permissive Action Links (PALs) on all nuclear weapons

A Permissive Action Link is an electro-mechanical device that prevents arming a nuclear warhead without receipt of a properly coded message. At this time all US Army and Air

Force nuclear weapons have PALs, but that is not true of Navy weapons. To what extent PALs are installed on Soviet, French and Chinese weapons is not known to us. As for British weapons, the situation presumably is the same as for the US. There was unanimous agreement that PALs should be installed on all nuclear weapons, irrespective of basing mode or nationality. In the case of the US, it would be important to do so on attack submarines, most particularly on their SLCMs and to a somewhat lesser degree on surface combatants, as these vessels are intended for operations in hostile environments. Ballistic missile submarines purposely operate in great isolation even in wartime, and are under a strict command regime, so the urgency for installing PALs on them is not as high.

Cooperative Measures

Four measures were proposed that received strong support:

1. PAL Information Exchange

The US (and presumably also the USSR and France) has invested appreciable resources over many years to developing PAL technologies. It would be in the US interest, and those of other states that have sophisticated PAL capabilities, to share this technology with other states.

2. C^3I Information Exchange

SALT and START have focused exclusively on weapons, and with the exception of certain limits on radars in the ABM treaty, have ignored C^3I. Given the vital importance of command, and growing mutual confidence, the US and Soviet militaries should begin systematic discussions regarding their command systems. These could educate both sides as to what peacetime (and perhaps crisis) activities are particularly dangerous. Such discussions could also lead to an enlargement of the 1989 Agreement on the Prevention of Dangerous Military Activities to cover space activities which should also receive serious consideration given that ASAT capabilities may be in the offing. Finally, in the long term, military-to-military discussions could facilitate agreements on operational constraints for strategic forces that would reduce risks in crisis.

3. Direct Links Between NORAD and its Counterparts

At this time the only US-USSR direct communication links are the Hot Line and the Risk Reduction Centers. While these are adequate for communication between the National Command Authorities in peacetime under normal circumstances, it is probably unlikely that they could transmit timely warning of an accidental launch before impact. Links between the commander of the US early warning system (NORAD) and the Soviet counterpart should be established with appropriate procedural filters to permit such communication only under well-defined contingencies.

4. Multinational Crisis Risk Reduction Center(s)

The capabilities embodied in the US/Soviet Hot Line and the new Risk Reduction Centers should be enlarged or replicated to form a global network incorporating all declared nuclear states, and possibly a larger set that would include the threshold states. This should be done under UN auspices, or on a multilateral basis, whichever is more expeditious and efficacious. At a minimum, the existing system should be enlarged to include China, France, and the UK.

The proposal was also made to place the superpowers' missile forces at a lower alert status in peacetime so as to reduce the risk of accidental launch, with the proviso that this be implemented in a verifiable manner. While no such technique was put forward short of separating warheads from boosters, it was proposed that further work on this idea should be undertaken. Some participants expressed a basic misgiving about this concept, however, for if the alert status were then raised in a crisis, this would convey a signal of extreme threat.

Accidents at High Alert Status

Obviously the risk that an accidental launch would lead to war is far greater in the context of a crisis sufficiently severe to stimulate a high level alert of nuclear forces (as during the Cuban Missile Crisis). For that reason most, and perhaps all, of the above measures would then take on far greater salience. In particular, PALs on naval vessels, and especially attack submarines, would be especially important, since these would then be operating in close proximity to the forces of the adversary, and/or be conducting highly intrusive intelligence missions, while operating only under one-way communications (and in the case of submarines, possibly communications silence). In the underseas environment, given the difficulties of acquiring reliable tactical information, the chances of miscalculation and accident are especially high. In this connection, particular concern was expressed in the conference that once American and Soviet submarines begin to confront each other during a crisis a tactical miscalculation or accident low in the chain of command could lead to an underwater Vincennes-type incident that might trigger accidental nuclear war.

Proposed measures specific to the high alert status environment, and not yet mentioned, include:

1. Reduced Reliance on (Elimination of) Prompt Launch

There was widespread agreement that the rather heavy reliance on prompt launch (i.e., launch-on-warning and launch-under-attack) apparently held by both superpowers poses a most dangerous risk to humanity, and that every effort must be made to reduce and eventually to remove it. The reason for this reliance is that both command systems are highly vulnerable to the adversary's strategic forces, while the fixed land-based forces are also very vulnerable. In consequence there would be pressure to launch while the command system is still functioning, which is opposed by the pressure to avoid nuclear war.

The pressure to launch promptly will only be relieved if the command systems, and to a lesser degree the forces, can survive attack and continue to function adequately. Several steps in this direction are already under way: the US Command-and-Control Improvement Program, [8] which is creating a command system that can survive a significantly heavier attack than its predecessor; and START, which will reduce the arsenals by about a third; and deployment of mobile ICBMs. But these will not suffice, though they will presumably raise the threshold for consideration of prompt launch. To attain the goal deeper cuts will be required to allow ongoing improvement in C^3I technologies [9] to win the race against the forces that could liquidate command; and to create forces that cannot be destroyed by preemption.

2. Operational Constraints on Ballistic Missile Submarines

Ballistic missiles launched by submarines patrolling near the US Atlantic coast and in the Norwegian Sea could hit Washington and Moscow, and other vital national command centers, in less than half the time that land-based ICBMs require for the same purpose [10]. To reduce the danger of surprise attack, and therefore the reliance on prompt launch, constraints on ballistic missile submarine operations have been proposed repeatedly, and were endorsed by all. These would forbid patrol by ballistic missile submarines within a specified distance of, say, Washington and Moscow, or perhaps in areas having a broader geographic definition. Such an agreement can be cooperatively verified [11].

3. ASAT Arms Control

Antisatellite (ASAT) weapons arms control was also strongly endorsed. Attacks on low orbit satellites could lead to escalation because of their importance in crisis and conventional war operations, not to mention that ASAT attacks might be (perhaps correctly) interpreted as an indicator that escalation was in prospect. ASAT use could thus contribute substantially to the creation of an environment that fosters accidental and/or inadvertent nuclear war. It should be noted, however, that unless very high performance directed energy weapons become available, the high-altitude satellites vital to strategic command are safe from surprise attack as rockets would

38

take several hours to reach them and thereby provide far earlier tactical warning than the launch of strategic weapons. To impede ASAT development, the most promising proposal is a treaty that would ban ASAT tests [12].

4. Removal of Ground-Based Tactical Nuclear Weapons

Ground-based nuclear weapons, especially nuclear-capable artillery, are arguably the most likely source of accidental use in a crisis, and in particular as it is appropriate to include conventional war under the rubric of crisis in the nuclear age. These weapons have a very cumbersome command system to prevent unauthorized use, and for that reason it is possible that circumstances could arise in which some level of predelegation would be authorized. At the same time, these weapons are likely to be enveloped by combat. Very strong (possibly unanimous) support was given to the proposition that if the Vienna negotiations are successful, and lead to conventional parity between NATO and the WTO, the two alliances should eliminate all ground-based nuclear weapons.

Accidental War Via Systemic Failure Modes of the Command System

The preceding discussion focused on the possibility that accidental (or unauthorized) launches could serve as triggers for accidental nuclear war, especially should the side subjected to such a launch respond with prompt launch. But risks that may be more grave, in part because they are less tangible, may lurk in the hardware/software systems that have become indispensable to military and political command organizations.

It is common knowledge that complex civil automated data handling and command systems (e.g., for use in commercial aviation), when first put into operation, are often plagued by bizarre malfunctions that were unforeseen and that are usually only resolved after protracted debugging. In the case of systems that are upgraded by elaboration and conglomeration over long periods of time, instead of wholesale redesign and replacement, there is the further problem that hardly any of the system's operators understand it in its entirety. In addition there is the problem of the ever-growing gap between the sophistication of such systems, and that of the bulk of its operators.

Both superpowers' strategic command systems rely on hardware/software systems of this character: they have been developed over decades, and because of their size must be staffed by personnel that, on the whole, are only trained to deal with a rather limited spectrum of circumstances. The sharpest contrast with civil systems, of course, is that these politico-military systems have **never** operated under the most highly stressing circumstances, such as both sides having placed their forces on a high alert status [13]. In that case, furthermore, they would no longer be two systems, because their mutual real-time interactions would have turned them, in effect, into a single complex. In peacetime it is only possible to test the system, and its personnel, to a limited degree by simulating such conditions. There is good reason, therefore, to be concerned that under highly stressing circumstances catastrophic failure modes could rear their heads.

By their nature, one cannot foresee how such failure modes would arise, but plausible scenarios are easily constructed. For example, under severe circumstances, tactical warning signals that the system's human component would reject as false in peacetime could, instead, open paths to large-scale failure modes because of the stress on those people, and/or the far larger data flow into the command system and the more rapid decision pace that it would be expected to meet [14].

The concern that their command system might malfunction under conditions in which it has never operated is one of the driving forces behind both militaries' interest in prompt launch. This provides yet another reason why the forces, command systems, and above all political structures, must be refashioned to make any real test of this whole system as remote a contingency as possible.

Hence, the possibility of accidental war being triggered by false warning that enemy missiles are on the way must be taken seriously even though in the past all potential false warnings in the US system have been clarified and rejected at some stage of the warning and/or decision-making process. (High-ranking Soviet military leaders have privately acknowledged that the Soviet Union, too, has experienced false warnings but that Soviet authorities have increased the dependability of their warning system and the reliability of their control system.)

It has to be understood that there are several steps in the process of identifying indicators of possible attack and in interpreting their significance and that, therefore, the term *false warning* is often applied very loosely and somewhat misleadingly to the initial stages of the process. An empirical study that found an apparent correlation between US policy makers' perception of increased tension in US-Soviet relations and the frequency of Threat Evaluation Conferences in the NORAD C^3I system was the subject of considerable discussion in the workshop since it seems to lend support to concerns that false warning is more likely during a tense crisis (see chapter IX). However, some questions were raised about certain aspects of the study and the causal significance of the correlation. It was agreed that follow-up research on this important subject is highly desirable.

Inadvertent War

Inadvertent war received less discussion in the workshop. In some usages, the term *inadvertent* refers to a scenario in which a crisis gets out of control and escalates to the point at which one or the other side (or both) come to believe that war is now inevitable and seemingly imminent, **and** that it is better to initiate a preemptive nuclear strike before the opponent does so. It is an unwanted war in that at the outset of the crisis neither side wanted or expected nuclear war but they drift and stumble into it as a result of provocative coercive bargaining, misperceptions, misjudgments and perhaps accidental or unauthorized actions, all of which feed escalation to the point at which conventional conflict might have begun and time-urgent decisions whether to preempt seem to be necessary [15]. (The emphasis here that inadvertent war could result from a crisis that escalates and spins out of control by no means implies that a crisis is not also one of the contexts in which an accidental war might take place.)

Many of the technical issues related to accidents that could contribute to crisis escalation that results in inadvertent war are already covered by the preceding discussion of accidental war, and the measures proposed there would, to a considerable degree, ameliorate the risk of inadvertent nuclear war. But this risk is fundamentally a political one since it depends on a decision to preempt made by top-level, responsible civilian authority.

Therefore everyone agrees that it is essential to avert conventional war for that would provide highly fertile ground for escalation leading to a possible preemptive strike. And by that token, it is also essential to prevent political differences from escalating into dangerous crises. The superpowers' behavior since the Cuban crisis indicates that they have grasped this point.

Measures that would reduce the risk of crisis escalation and the outbreak of conventional war between nuclear armed states must, in consequence of the preceding observation, be largely political. The Confidence and Security Building Measures (CSBM) regime now under discussion at Vienna shows the promise of creating a truly new situation which would substantially reduce the dangers inherent in the following dilemma: prudent defensive preparations based on pessimistic assessment of an opponent's intentions could be misperceived as a signal of impending attack, and thus provoke preemption, whereas failure to take such precautions could invite attack. At the moment there is still little thought on, let alone movement towards, CSBM that would serve the same purpose in the strategic confrontation. This is an area that warrants further work. The ballistic missile submarine standoff zone, and a set of CSBM that would constrain military operations in space as part of an ASAT arms control regime, are two possibilities that were already mentioned.

Effects of Crisis-Induced Stress
on Decision Making [16]

"That kind of crisis-induced pressure [during the Cuban missile crisis] does strange things to a human being, even to brilliant, self-confident, mature, experienced men. For some it brings out characteristics and strengths that perhaps even they never knew they had, and for others the pressure is too overwhelming" [17].

"I saw first-hand, during the long days and nights of the Cuban crisis, how brutally physical and mental fatigue can numb the good sense as well as the senses of normally articulate men" [18].

A former high official in the Kennedy administration was asked several years ago to clarify these cryptic observations made by Robert Kennedy and Theodore Sorensen. He replied that two important members of the President's advisory group had been unable to cope with the stress of the crisis; they became quite passive and were unable to fulfill their responsibilities. Their condition was very noticeable, however, and others took over their duties. Inability to cope with crisis-induced stress has been reported for other leaders as well: Stalin after the Nazi attack on the Soviet Union, Prime Minister Anthony Eden at the time of the Suez crisis in 1956, Israeli Army Chief of Staff Yitzhak Rabin during the 1967 Middle East crisis, India's Jawaharlal Nehru in 1962 and Egypt's Gamal Abdel Nasser in 1967.

In these cases the dysfunctional effects of stress on the policymaker were highly visible and could be easily recognized by others, thus providing opportunities for timely intervention and compensatory action by others. But, as will be noted, extreme stress can also have less visible and therefore more insidious effects on the performance of decision-making tasks.

A great deal is known about the effects of stress on the performance of a variety of tasks. A mild level of stress generally improves an individual's or a group's performance but as stress increases to higher levels and/or is prolonged performance worsens. The point at which this cross-over occurs varies for different individuals and groups so that, fortunately, one would expect — as in the Cuban missile crisis — some members of a decision-making group to continue to function effectively even though the performance of others has sharply deteriorated.

The following is a brief summary of the major types of harmful effects of extreme stress on performance of complex cognitive tasks of the kind associated with crisis decision-making. Most of these effects are of the insidious, not the easily recognizable kind referred to above:

1. **Impaired attention and perception**: (a) important aspects of the crisis situation may escape scrutiny; (b) conflicting values and interests at stake may be overlooked; (c) the range of perceived action alternatives is likely to narrow but not necessarily to the best option; and (d) the search for relevant information and options tends to be dominated by past experience, with a tendency to fall back on familiar solutions that have worked in the past, whether or not they are appropriate to the present situation.

2. **Increased cognitive rigidity**: (a) impaired ability to improvise and reduced creativity in problem-solving; (b) reduced receptivity to information that challenges existing beliefs and preferences; (c) increased stereotypic thinking; and (d) reduced tolerance of ambiguity, which results in a tendency to cut off information search and option evaluation and to make decisions prematurely.

3. **Shortened and narrowed perspectives**: (a) less attention to longer-range consequences of options; (b) less attention to side-effects of options.

4. **Shifting the burden to the opponent:** (a) belief that one's own options for dealing with the crisis and avoiding escalation are quite limited, and (b) belief that only the opponent has it within his power to prevent an impending disaster.

The emotional climate of crisis decision-making (anger, fear, distrust) exacerbates these tendencies, contributes to misperceptions and misjudgments, and may provide impulses for immediate strong action of some kind. Under certain conditions decision-making groups that enjoy strong group cohesion may attempt to cope with the cognitive and moral stresses experienced in a crisis by engaging in concurrence-seeking, avoiding challenges to each other and providing mutual support, thus falling victim to the phenomenon of *groupthink*.

Responsibility for shielding the decision-making process from the adverse effects of stress on some members of the group must be shared by its members. There must be a willingness and a capacity to recognize when some individual or the group as a whole is no longer able to handle the psychological stress, the emotional and physical fatigue of a tense crisis. In addition, methods and techniques for stress avoidance and stress management need to be incorporated into the procedures of the policymaking system and, indeed, into the medical support system available to top officials.

There is almost universal consensus among specialists on decision-making as to *standards and practices* that a decision-making group should adhere to in processing information, generating alternative courses of action, and evaluating options before decisions are made. These standards are well known and need not be repeated here. Suffice to say that adherence to such good decision-making practices will itself help to reduce possibly dysfunctional effects of stress. But for such benefits to be realized these standards must be imbedded in the norms of the policy-making group; they must be internalized by all participants; and the decision-making process in a crisis must be carefully monitored by the executive and/or a surrogate charged with this responsibility (i.e., the *custodian-manager* of the process) in order to spot possibly serious deviations from these norms and practices and to take corrective action on a timely basis.

In addition, the amount and quality of *preparatory work* (i.e., anticipating and analyzing a variety of hypothetical crises) has been shown to be important in reducing the dysfunctional effects of stress. While crisis simulations on a classified basis are known to take place at a relatively high level in the US government (and perhaps in the Soviet government), participation seldom extends to the top leaders who will be called upon to make the critically important decisions in crises. And the focus of such crisis simulations seems to be directed more to improvement of policy planning than to generating the kinds of preparatory work that could reduce vulnerability to stress or increase familiarity with and practice in applying crisis management precepts.

Effects of Organic Illness and Sleep Deprivation on Decision Making

The possibility that major psychiatric impairment in a key official may not be detected or controlled in time to prevent a policy disaster and that crisis-induced stress may activate latent psychological vulnerabilities or psychotic tendencies in an individual are matters of legitimate and grave concern. However, these possible sources of accidental or inadvertent nuclear war were not singled out for discussion in our conference.

Some attention, however, was given to the effects that various organic illnesses, emotional and physical fatigue, and sleep deprivation can have on crisis decision-making. Medical problems such as heart disease, strokes, traumas, surgery, cancer, hypertension, blood loss are known to produce deficits in the afflicted individual's performance of various cognitive functions — such as the ability to concentrate, the span of attention, memory, inventiveness, deductive and inductive reasoning, etc. A manifest overlap exists between cognitive effects of organic disease and those of extreme stress that were alluded to above. Illness can heighten vulnerability to crisis-induced stress. Moreover, insufficient attention has been given to the likelihood that the side effects of many medications can contribute to impairment of cognitive functioning.

It is of critical importance to establish and make timely use of procedures for identifying temporarily disabled heads of state and other key officials and removing them from their primary decision-making role. Clarification and rehearsal of such procedures should occur from the first days of a new administration and repeated periodically.

Pronounced sleep deprivation and disruption of an individual's circadian rhythms (i.e., the *biological clock*) can also result in impaired cognitive functioning. This problem can arise also with odd sleep cycles that are in conflict with a human being's natural circadian system, possibly resulting in insomnia, emotional disturbance, impaired information processing and judgment. (It has been reported that pronounced sleep deprivation of key individuals contributed to the faulty decision-making process that led to the Challenger accident.)

After a day or two of sleep deprivation, stimulant medication, such as amphetamines, has been shown to reverse most of the documented performance impairment. This might be useful in a short-term situation, but the harmful potential of prolonged use of stimulants by crisis decision-makers and other key personnel in the chain of command would be especially troublesome in the nuclear era for it risks inducing a paranoid state-of-mind accompanied by greatly heightened impulsiveness and very poor judgment.

The medical support system available to top policymakers in the past has functioned erratically and at times inadequately. This system should be periodically reviewed and upgraded as necessary to provide comprehensive quality care not only for the treatment of organic illness and careful monitoring for possibly adverse side-effects of medications; in addition it should provide effective monitoring and advice with regard to dysfunctional effects of extreme stress, avoidance of debilitating fatigue from overwork and inadequate sleep, and appropriate counselling with respect to the adverse effects of over reliance on sleeping pills and amphetamines.

Crisis Management and Crisis Avoidance

As noted earlier, maintaining the quality of the decision-making process during a crisis is one way of providing safeguards against the harmful impact of psychological stress, organic illness, sleep deprivation, emotional and physical fatigue. Another way is to ensure that participants in the decision-making group are thoroughly familiar with the general principles and requirements of crisis management and have acquired appropriate training to equip them to deal with the challenging task of applying these general principles to the special characteristics of a particular crisis that they are forced to deal with.

To be sure, all past superpower crises were managed and terminated without any kind of shooting war between US and Soviet forces and, indeed, there has not been a war-threatening superpower confrontation since the October 1973 war in the Middle East, and even in that sole instance the danger of war was remote [19]. Nonetheless, we believe that the possibility of additional superpower crises of a war-threatening nature cannot be ignored, and that there is no guarantee that crisis management efforts would be equally successful in the future. In fact, developments of the past decade in military systems and deployment have raised serious questions among informed observers as to whether crisis management concepts and procedures would be robust enough to withstand the escalatory pressures inherent in any new superpower confrontation.

Given the widely shared view that if nuclear war occurs — whether accidental or inadvertent — it is likely to do so during the course of a tense superpower confrontation, the highest priority must be given to continuing efforts to avoid war-threatening crises and to strengthening crisis management capabilities. In the limited space available only a few suggestions can be offered.

1. When conflicts of interest are simmering, threatening to erupt into a dangerous crisis, the superpowers should rely in the first instance on timely diplomatic communication and negotiation rather than engage in efforts to protect their interests by unilateral actions that are likely to provoke counter moves and crisis escalation.

2. In peacetime as well as when embroiled in a dispute the superpowers should avoid sudden and/or secret military deployments that affect the strategic or regional military

balance; and they should forego foreign policy initiatives that seek to make major gains at each other's expense. Unless American and Soviet leaders observe such restraints in their behavior towards each other, high-sounding declarations that they will forego use of force and threats of force against each other will remain hollow and brittle.

3. Control and restraint of one's military forces is a critical requirement for effective crisis management. Top-level leaders on both sides must exercise informed and judicious control over all movements and alerts of combat forces. Leaders must be sensitive to and deal constructively with the tension that frequently exists in crisis situations between the imperatives of military logic and the requirements of diplomacy if they are to prevent unwanted escalation in crisis situations. Similarly, it is of the utmost importance that the rules of engagement given to combat forces be carefully chosen and monitored to reduce and control the risks of unwanted escalation.

4. When a war-threatening crisis erupts each side may find it necessary to take measures to reduce the vulnerability of its theatre forces and to enhance its readiness to defend itself. However, at the same time, American and Soviet leaders should take the greatest care to avoid alerts and deployments that are likely to be perceived by the other side as preparations for significant and imminent *offensive* operations. They should also avoid (or at least greatly minimize) the practice of using military alerts and deployments to signal resolution and/or to exert coercive pressure on the adversary for crisis bargaining purposes. In brief, there should be more use of diplomatic communication and less reliance on military signalling per se.

5. The task of crisis management should not focus exclusively on avoiding an accidental or inadvertent nuclear war only in the circumstance when a crisis has already escalated to high-level alerts. However important it is to increase the reliability of warning systems, to eliminate the possibility of launch on false warning, to avoid or

neutralize the effect of accidental or unauthorized actions and human errors, etc.; etc., elementary prudence demands that maximal efforts be made to prevent a conflict of interest from developing into a tense US-Soviet crisis which will severely test their ability to avoid accidental or inadvertent war. Accordingly, the first objective of crisis management should be to terminate any US-Soviet crisis promptly and effectively at its outset before it is allowed to escalate to dangerously high levels. US and Soviet leaders should discuss with each other in peace-time ways of preventing crisis escalation in different contexts, including regional conflicts in which they are supporting rival regional actors.

6. The time factor may be critical if efforts to avoid escalation and terminate a crisis are to have an opportunity to succeed. Accordingly, leaders on both sides must recognize the necessity to slow down the tempo and momentum of crisis developments. They may need to deliberately create pauses in crisis activity — as, for example, President Kennedy did in the Cuban missile crisis — in order to provide enough time for the two sides to exchange diplomatic communications and to give the leadership on both sides adequate time to assess the situation, make well-considered decisions, respond to each other's proposals, etc.

7. Limitation of the objectives one pursues in a confrontation with the other superpower and resisting the temptation to inflict a damaging, humiliating defeat on the opponent may be essential if a superpower crisis is to be settled without escalation to dangerously high alert levels. While seeking to protect its own fundamental interests, each side must recognize the other side's legitimate interests and strive for a mutually acceptable formula for terminating the crisis.

8. A great deal of essential knowledge and relevant experience has been gained from managing past US-Soviet crises successfully. But the learning experience is virtually worthless unless the lessons and requisite skills are codified

and institutionalized in each government. This body of knowledge and know-how must be transmitted quickly and effectively to new leaders and staff members who will have important crisis management responsibilities. It must be internalized by them via appropriate training, exercises, and rehearsals so that they will perform effectively the very first time they are called upon to manage a crisis.

9. Finally, since effective control and management of US-Soviet confrontations may depend critically on the ability of the two sides to avoid misperceptions and miscalculations and to communicate rapidly and effectively with each other, it is highly desirable for Soviet and American military and civilian specialists to discuss together problems of crisis stability, to identify types of behaviors that may threaten loss of control and trigger escalation pressures, and to consider and make provision for preventive and remedial measures.

Managing and Improving
the Overall US-Soviet Relationship

Members of the conference emphasized that the state of overall US-Soviet political relations is a contextual factor that influences whether accidental and unauthorized military actions and events stemming from human error and frailty will contribute to processes that lead to accidental or inadvertent war. Progress in arms control cannot proceed expeditiously and in fuller measure except in conjunction with improvement in the overall relationship.

During the past forty years US and Soviet leaders have developed and generally adhered to a number of fundamental though largely tacit *rules of prudence* and this has helped to limit the conflict potential of their relationship, even during its most tense periods. These tacit rules should be discussed, clarified, elaborated, and strengthened. They include, but are not limited to the following [20]:

(1) Respect and do not challenge each other's vital interests; this rule has an important corollary: avoid provocative efforts to exploit difficulties the other

superpower is having in its sphere of influence or in its efforts to withdraw from advanced positions in the Third World.

(2) Do not initiate military action of any kind against the other superpower's military forces. Whatever the likelihood that even low-level conventional military clashes could escalate to nuclear war, the risk is not acceptable. This rule of prudence was recognized and endorsed in the joint communiqué issued by Reagan and Gorbachev at their first summit in 1985: "Recognizing that any conflict between the USSR and the US could have catastrophic consequences, they emphasized the importance of preventing any war between them, whether nuclear or conventional."

(3) In superpower crises (such as in Berlin, Cuba and the Middle East in the past), do not exploit an advantage to the point that the other side is forced to make the awesome choice between accepting a humiliating diplomatic defeat or initiating use of military force in order to prevent such a setback;

(4) When the two superpowers are backing rival regional actors in a Third Area conflict (e.g., the Middle East), each superpower should accept responsibility for preventing its regional ally from inflicting a shattering defeat on the regional ally of the other superpower, thereby placing that superpower in the position of having to intervene. If a superpower is unable or unwilling to discharge its responsibility to restrain its victorious ally, it should accept the necessity for the other superpower's intervention as a last resort to prevent its regional ally from suffering such a defeat.

These tacit rules of prudence need to be supplemented by more explicit *rules of cooperation* in the interest of developing a more constructive and stable bilateral relationship and a safer and more viable global society. The superpowers should seek to reach agreements that will enable them to deal more effectively with predictably sensitive and potentially explosive situations that affect not only their own well-being but that of other peoples as well. They should strengthen existing procedures and create new institutional mechanisms to address the variety of issues that already are or could become highly dangerous to peace, that are corrosive of their overall relationship or harmful to the global community. They should increase efforts to develop better understanding and communication between political and military leaders and officials at all levels in the interest of creating *a sense of partnership* for dealing with these threats.

The Soviet Union and the United States have already made substantial progress in developing a variety of cooperative arrangements for enhancing their security. Leaders on both sides have gradually come to understand that they can no longer assure the security of their own country at acceptable cost and risk through strictly unilateral national efforts as in the past. The realization that each superpower is dependent for its security on the behavior of the other — i.e., a condition of mutual vulnerability and mutual dependence — has provided powerful incentives for security cooperation. Both superpowers are moving towards a realization that the traditional conception of *national security* must be broadened to include a new conception of *mutual security.*

Under changing conditions that create new challenges but also offer new opportunities, *theories of cooperation and conflict resolution* formulated by psychologists, game theorists and other specialists assume enhanced practical import. Foreign policy officials in both countries should acquire thorough familiarity with these theories and should consider how they can be adapted and utilized in efforts to develop a more constructive and stable US-Soviet relationship and a more viable and livable global society.

Notes

[1] What *accidental* and *inadvertent* war have in common is that neither is a *premeditated* war, as exemplified by the classical *preventive war*. In the modern era, the preventive war option is associated with the hypothetical possibility that one of the superpowers might plan and

initiate an unprovoked nuclear war, most likely under peacetime conditions in order to achieve surprise, so as to destroy its opponent's war-making potential and to eliminate or sharply reduce its ability to compete in the international arena. Preventive war was excluded from our discussion.

[2] The distinction between launch-on-warning (LOW) and launch-under-attack (LUA) is not as clearcut as is often supposed. First, it is likely that one or more high-altitude nuclear bursts that only produce electrical disturbances (EMP) would precede detonations that cause any permanent damage or casualties; and it is unclear whether the victim of the attack would consider such detonations to be part of strategic warning, or confirmation of an attack (i.e., tactical warning). Second, it is likely that LOW would only get under way after at least some enemy warheads had detonated on their targets. Third, presumably there are thresholds for the size of an attack below which prompt launch would surely be ruled out, and that for attacks above threshold the response would depend on a variety of factors. Among the latter would be the degree of confidence in the ability of the command systems to characterize and assess the attack in question promptly.

[3] The conviction that preemption is an irrational option even if unambiguous strategic warning appears to be in hand, combined with the fear that a coordinated counterattack could not be carried out after a major first strike had been fully absorbed, has apparently driven the US (and in all likelihood the Soviet Union) to place increased reliance on prompt launch despite the many chilling drawbacks entailed in this option (see Kurt Gottfried and Bruce G. Blair, eds, **Crisis Stability and Nuclear War** (New York: Oxford University Press, 1988) pp. 83-89). Nevertheless, one cannot be fully certain that a policy adopted in peacetime will survive the inhuman pressures that would attend decision making should a strategic exchange ever appear to be imminent.

[4] Unless otherwise stated, it is taken for granted that *accidental launch* includes subsequent detonation on a target of value.

[5] This situation is illustrated by the Middle East Crisis of 1973. In this case the USSR did not raise its readiness, while the US briefly staged a limited global alert, in part because it wanted quickly to convey a political signal by means of the alert order for this produces a burst in message traffic that Soviet electronic intelligence would immediately recognize.

[6] See especially Sherman Frankel, "Negating Accidental or Unauthorized Launches of Nuclear Weapons" I/P Report No. 89-01 (unpublished) June, 1989, Physics Department, University of Pennsylvania, Philadelphia, PA 19104.

[7] As to the technical dimension, it might not be feasible to install CDC on reentry vehicles because of the weight penalty, but that problem would not arise for the MIRV bus or the booster

[8] The essential elements are high-altitude communications satellites (MILSTAR), a radio network for transmitting emergency action messages throughout the US (GWEN), and ground-mobile command centers and communication nodes. All are designed to function in a nuclear environment .

[9] An important improvement would be more accurate and quicker attack assessment. This might be a (the only ?) benefit of the effort to develop a space-based ABM system.

[10] For a typical strategic attack scenario, see Ashton B. Carter, John D. Steinbruner and Charles A. Zraket, eds, **Managing Nuclear Operations** (Washington: Brookings, 1987) p. 580.

[11] Gottfried and Blair, eds, op. cit. pp. 302-3.

[12] Ibid., pp. 98-101, 303-304.

[13] By *high alert status* we mean some significant fraction of the following: the wartime backup command systems in operation, most missile submarines at sea, a large portion of the bomber fleet on strip alert, and appreciable rise in readiness of non-strategic forces. In the case of the US this would correspond to DEFCON 2, or at least a fully generated DEFCON 3. The 1973 alert was a very attenuated DEFCON 3; during the Cuban crisis SAC (but no other command) was at DEFCON 2 which is the only

time that such a high state of readiness was invoked since the centrally coordinated Defense Condition (DEFCON) system was established in view of the disastrous failure of the alerting system at Pearl Harbor. (SAC is at DEFCON 4 in peacetime, whereas all other US commands are then at DEFCON 5; DEFCON 1 can be taken as tantamount to strategic warning of imminent attack, or deployment for combat.)

[14] By the same token, an accidental launch that would be recognized as such in peacetime might in a severe crisis stimulate a catastrophic response because of systemic malfunction.

[15] Historical instances of war that neither side expected or wanted at the beginning of a crisis provide other scenarios of inadvertent war which are less relevant to our immediate discussion.

[16] This section, it will be noted, refers only to the effects of stress on high level decision makers. The effects of stress on persons at lower levels of responsibility is discussed in detail by Abrams (see chapter X).

[17] Robert F, Kennedy, **Thirteen Days; A Memoir of the Cuban Missile Crisis** (W.W. Norton, 1971) p. 22.

[18] Theodore C. Sorensen, **Decision-Making in the White House** (Columbia University Press, 1964) p. 76.

[19] Raymond L. Garthoff, **Detente and Confrontation: from Nixon to Reagan** (Washington: Brookings, 1985), chapter 11; Gottfried and Blair, op. cit., pp. 198-206.

[20] For additional discussion see G. T. Allison, W. L. Ury, and B. J. Allyn, eds. **Windows of Opportunity: From Cold War to Peaceful Competition in US-Soviet Relations** (Cambridge, MA, 1989); Chapter 1, "Primitive Rules of Prudence," by Graham T. Allison.

IV. Component Failure in the Military and Accidental Nuclear War

Herbert L. Abrams

For analytic purposes, the term *accidental* may be used to describe a series of *triggers* that may precipitate or interact with events to produce nuclear war. The technical-mechanical triggers fit into well-defined categories:

1. Nuclear weapons accidents, including accidental launches.
2. Accidents to weapons transport systems, such as aircraft, submarines and ships.
3. Command and control malfunction, including computer breakdown, signal misinterpretation, and power failure.
4. Sensing systems errors, with consequent false warnings.
5. Automated decision making. A false warning perceived as an attack by a country that has moved to *launch-on-warning* is potentially the most clearcut prelude to *accidental* nuclear war.

While human error may affect all aspects of the complex systems that govern the great-power nuclear forces, component failure characterizes virtually all systems accidents [1]. Furthermore, a series of failures is frequently involved. Without knowledge of component reliability, it is impossible to analyze the robustness of a system as a whole [2].

In a conference focussed on the relationship of command and control systems — or military systems as a class — to the possibility of unintended nuclear war, the potential failure of components that comprise complex systems surely requires consideration.

Background

All parts ultimately fail. When this occurs at an anticipated rate, systems will generally accommodate to failure if design is optimal, or can be prevented from failing by the periodic replacement of parts. Beyond the range of statistical expectation, faulty components may initiate a chain of events so disruptive that neither redundancy nor safeguards can preclude system breakdown. This is true in spite of the fact that complex systems are designed to accommodate to and compensate for some degree of component failure.

A part fails in an electronic system when its strength is less than the stress imposed on it [3]. Variations in failure rates are found within three life stages of components. In the first stage, known as the **infant mortality period**, the population characteristically exhibits a high failure rate. Early failures are largely attributable to deficiencies in design, shoddy construction, transportation damage, and improper installation. Poor welds or seals, weak connections, dirt or contamination on surfaces or in materials, and incorrect positioning of parts are a few examples. Such failures may be reduced by greater control over the manufacturing process, improvements in design or materials, and emphasis on factory tests and reliability systems [4].

Once the weaker units have been eliminated, the failure rate can be stabilized at a relatively low level. This stage is called the **useful life period**. Failures in this phase stem largely from stress-related factors, such as humidity, temperature cycling, vibration, thermal or mechanical shock, and conditions at high altitudes, initiated largely by chance [5].

The final stage, known as the **wearout period**, demonstrates a rapidly rising failure rate. Most problems during this phase are attributable to weakening of the design strength of an item, reflecting long-term environmental and operational stresses. Deterioration stems from factors such as corrosion, oxidation, frictional wear, and shrinkage or cracking in plastics. Such failures can be minimized by replacing parts before an unacceptably high wearout level occurs [6].

Reliability in military operations is complicated by factors not seen in commercial or industrial applications. Non-military applications usually incorporate state-of-the-art components with a proven record of reliability, whereas military applications often require a higher performance level. In order to get this high performance, advanced technology may be used before its reliability has been fully tested. Furthermore, military systems may operate in extremely harsh environments that extend the capabilities of equipment beyond normal limits [7].

The systems may be degraded further through operational abuses such as rough handling of equipment, extended duty cycles, and neglected maintenance. Once in the field, the reliability of spare parts cannot be guaranteed. Some systems may be repaired with unspecified parts or parts from a variety of different manufacturers [8].

Causes of Electronic Component Failure

Electronic components are subject to many problems. Integrated circuits (ICs) may not be hermetically sealed, making them "time bombs waiting to cause failures in the field" [9]. An industry examination of integrated circuit producers found widespread failure to check the packaging of their ICs after electrical testing and test procedures that actually broke the hermetic seals. Another analysis determined that package seal defects caused 23% of all integrated circuit failures in military electronics [10].

Electronic components are subject to a wide range of environmental stresses. Excessively high temperatures are a common source of mishaps in military electronic equipment, causing melted solder joints, solid state device burn out, and chemical degradation [11].

Low temperature, while decreasing chemical degeneration, can also cause major problems. Defects from low temperature are usually associated with the mechanical elements of a system. Breakdown stems from the expansion of metallic and non-metallic materials, the freezing of entrapped moisture, and the stiffening of liquid constituents [12]. The brittleness of a seal at low temperature was a major factor leading to its failure in the Challenger disaster of January, 1986.

Sudden temperature changes can create significant mechanical stress as well. Humidity and salt air promote corrosion in metallic components. Performance can be degraded by electromagnetic and nuclear radiation. Vibration, shock, low pressure, sand, and dust may all predispose parts to fail in an exacting environment [13].

The testing of microchips is a special problem. Nearly all producers use a procedure called *burn-in*, which subjects chips to elevated temperatures and permits identification of potential early failures in the first 100 hours of use [14]. Yet this method cannot prevent electromigration, in which the aluminum in circuit components rearranges itself under electrical stress. Burn-in may actually accelerate the process, reducing a chip's lifetime significantly. The Pave Paws radar experienced such rapid electromigration that multiple circuit replacement was required each week during one period [15].

Failure can occur in any component of a semiconductor — in the capsule, the macrochip, the chip attachment, the wire bonds, the aluminum conductors, and the bulk silicon [16].

A View of the Record

What kind of performance have our contractors achieved? Clearly, there are large areas in the military in which both weapons and communication systems, carefully designed and produced, function optimally. Nevertheless, the past decade — and previous periods — have demonstrated major lapses in quality that require attention. The use of selective examples demonstrates that our focus on statistical failure must be broadened to include certain systematic deficiencies of design, construction, testing, etc., that heighten the risk of failure. Whether due to shoddiness or deliberate irresponsibility, reliability problems undermine the effectiveness and dependability of the military system as a whole.

What we are primarily concerned with are failures that might raise the risk of accidental war. Observation systems, early warning systems, and command, control and intelligence systems are the obvious ones which would require a sustained high level of performance to minimize the risk. These are not systems deployed in large numbers so as to supply us with good statistics on failure. Hence, many of the examples of documented failure that have come to light deal with weapons' problems. But these systems are procured by the same procedures, paid for by the same budgets, and frequently produced by the same manufacturers as the systems crucial to accidental war prevention.

In 1982, the General Accounting Office (GAO) reported that the cruise missile had failed major tests of reliability, maintainability, mission suitability, or ability to reach its target [17]. The GAO found that the missile suffered serious engine deficiencies, might be unable to survive Soviet defenses, could not effectively attack certain target types, and lacked a guidance system for attacking most targets in certain areas [18].

In 1983, the Army Chief of Staff, General John A. Wickham, Jr., stated that all five failures in 16 Pershing II flight tests were caused by shoddy construction. Missing shims (washers), a failed casing joint, a faulty hydraulic pump, and two short circuits resulted in test failures [19].

In 1984, a series of weapons defects was disclosed. The Navy discovered cracks in the tails of F-18 fighter planes produced by McDonnell Douglas Corporation. A design problem caused powerful spiraling air currents to shake the tail fins under certain flight conditions, cracking the tails [20].

Production of Phoenix air-to-air missiles was temporarily halted when navy inspectors dismantled one of the missiles produced by Hughes Aircraft Company. The inspection revealed extremely poor quality control [21].

Soon afterwards, two more Hughes-produced weapons were found to have such serious deficiencies that the Army and Air Force refused to accept them. The rejected weapons were TOW (tube-launched, optically tracked, wire-guided) anti-tank missiles and Maverick air-to-surface missiles [22].

The TOW missiles suffered a unique problem: one in a thousand would fall to the ground after being fired, then take off again, unguided. The problem was caused by cold solder joints between the battery and the rest of the missile's electrical system. With the recommendation of Hughes that the army not take corrective action (it would be too costly), the TOW, as of 1982, was still produced at a rate of 1000 per month [23].

After a series of testing problems with the Division Air Defense Gun (DIVAD), the Pentagon finally cancelled development because of test failures and poor reliability [24]. Internal air force reports pointed to similar deficiencies in the Advanced Medium Range air-to-air missile (AMRAAM), casting doubt on whether it could be produced effectively [25].

In January, 1986, the Army discovered cracks in the main rotary blades in 13 of its 68 AH-64 Apache helicopters. The Army grounded its Apache fleet until the completion of an investigation into the causes of the cracks [26].

In August, 1987 serious problems with the guidance system of the MX Missile were described by the House Armed Services Committee. The concern was about the performance of the system's inertial measurement unit. Some elements of the system had not been tested properly and parts had been purchased outside of approved procurement channels. Only five of seventeen test flights used missiles equipped with the production version of the guidance system; in three, the accuracy was below average. Two fell outside their target area. Northrup falsely certified that a component of the inertial measurement unit worked to specifications. The company accepted faulty parts from subcontractors and charged the government for repairing them [27].

In October, 1987 the Deputy Inspector of the Defense Department, reporting the use of inferior materials by contractors, stated that "Product substitution is the most important law enforcement problem confronting the Pentagon in fraud related cases." The Defense Criminal Investigative Service had brought product substitution charges against eighty-five companies since January, 1986, and had 231 cases under advisement [28].

On March 21, 1989, in its first undersea launching, the 25 million dollar Trident 2 missile exploded four seconds after it was launched by a submarine off Cape Canaveral. It was the missile's third failure since January, 1988. The cause was thought to be a faulty control nozzle [29].

On March 28, 1989, 97 B-1 bombers were grounded after the movable wing on one of the planes swung too far forward and punctured a fuel tank, two and a half years after the plane was introduced. It was not clear whether the failure was mechanical or electrical. Three B-1 bombers crashed between September 1987 and November 1988. The B-1 continues to exhibit deficiencies in its radar jamming devices [30].

On April 11, Northrup was indicted on 167 counts, charged with knowingly supplying navigation devices that would freeze at a temperature higher than demanded by Air Force specifications [31].

On May 19, 1989, Robert Costello, the Under Secretary for Defense who had resigned the previous week, recommended cancelling the Stealth bomber because of high cost and the absence of an adequate quality control program. Costello characterized Northrup's quality control on the project as "terrible" [32].

Electronic components play a critical role in many military systems and have special reliability needs [33]. The Pentagon spends many billions of dollars on semiconductors alone [34]. Failure of these elements can have serious consequences, as shown by the false warnings in June 1980, caused by a defective computer chip [35]. Numerous problems have been uncovered.

A Titan III launch vehicle was found to have defective transistors. Unattached conductive particles in a power transistor package caused the failure of the guidance system, which in turn resulted in the loss of the delivery vehicle and payload [36].

The National Semiconductor Corporation pleaded guilty to defrauding the government by selling the DOD defective computer chips (which were installed in the B-1 bomber, M-1 tank, F-18 fighter aircraft, and the space shuttle) between 1978 and 1981 [37].

In 1984, the Air Force discovered that up to 15 million semiconducters purchased from IBM were inadequately tested by the manufacturer, Texas Instruments. The chips, produced over the previous eight years, were used in over 270 weapons systems, including the B-52 and Bl-B bombers and the F-15 fighter, as well as the space shuttle [38-40].

A few months later, a third microchip producer, Fairchild Camera and Instrument Company, informed the Pentagon that the chips it sold to defense contractors may have been improperly tested. The components were used in aircraft and radar, as well as other equipment [41].

The evidence indicates that the reliability of some military or space systems has been degraded by defective electronics. Faulty Texas Instrument circuits caused IBM computer failures on space shuttle flights in 1983 and 1984, according to NASA's Director of Reliability [42].

Other Factors in Component Failure

Quite aside from the anticipated life cycle of components, several other factors underlie the failure of military parts. Corporations competing for weapons contracts make exaggerated promises about performance, quality, and costs [43].

Once the Pentagon has selected the prime contractor, agency officials develop a vested interest in promoting the weapons system to higher Pentagon offices and Congress. "The services and their corporate suppliers, therefore, share incentives to overstate likely performance, understate costs, and underestimate technological risk" [44].

DOD agencies may fail to specify the precise level of reliability required for a particular system. The agencies may not have set criteria for the mean time between failures or the speed with which the system should be repairable. This lack of clarity hampers purchasing agencies in determining whether a given contractor is capable of manufacturing the system [45].

The function of a component may not be precisely defined during the crucial early design phases. A Navy study a few years ago showed that most failures in naval electronic equipment could be traced to poorly designed and manufactured power supplies. Designers often are not aware of what the power supply is supposed to deliver until relatively late in the design process [46].

Reliability is often of lower priority than other goals, such as performance, expense, and maintaining the production schedule [47]. The focus is on high performance and technological innovation rather than the stodgier values of reliability and maintainability (RAM). When a budget sacrifice must be made, program managers tend to shortchange reliability. Those with a greater stake in RAM, such as logistics and field commands, have little input in the design and production decision process [48].

It is not surprising, therefore, that a major cause of component fallibility is contractors' failure to design for quality from the start. Now, with widespread recognition of these failures, a greater emphasis has been placed on designing for reliability and maintenance on the drawing board [49-51].

In November 1985, the Semiconducter Industry Association criticized government procurement practices because they emphasize testing for quality after semiconducters are produced rather than building quality into the design [52]. NASA has found design problems to be the major cause of unreliability in spacecraft performance, with 42% of all determined component failures resulting from design errors [53].

Once a system has been designed and produced, inadequate selection and testing of components contributes to failure. For electronic components, a supplier may provide insufficient testing or none at all. Even if a supplier is found to be testing inadequately, purchasing may simply be cut off for a short period and soon resumed [54]. The Army Chief of Staff has indicated that problems with weapons systems stem from poor quality control by contractors. This one factor may elevate weapons costs by 30 to 80% [55].

Once a component is put into active use, it is subject to a new array of reliability problems. Equipment and systems reliabilities during actual service are one third to one tenth the level predicted during design [56].

The poor design of the cruise missile engine and guidance system, cracks in the tails of fighter planes, or faulty microchips may not trigger major catastrophe in themselves, but the prevalence of these problems raises serious questions.

If defective microchips can produce false warnings and if thousands of imperfect chips are implanted in the nuclear weapons systems and C^3I, how can we predict the reliability of systems essential to stability in crisis?

Improving Component Reliability

Excess defense funding has been considered one factor in problems of poor quality control, rushed production, and unforeseen design failures. Defense contractors overwhelmed with orders suffer from heavy production demands, so that quality and reliability suffer. The free flow of defense dollars may discourage reform of wasteful or abusive practices [57] and encourage spending on dubious weapons systems [58].

The fostering of competition has been repeatedly endorsed as a means of improving quality and reducing waste [59]. The Packard Commission Report recommended "substantially increased use of commercial style competition, emphasizing quality and established performance, as well as price" [60]. Congress now requires *dual sourcing* for the development and production of weapons. The services must develop two or more sources of production for weapons programs costing over a billion dollars, as long as this is cost-effective and will not delay the program. Nevertheless, the evidence is far from compelling that competition has achieved its goals in military research and development [61]. In particular, it does not appear to be cost-effective when hardware is sparingly produced or frequently redesigned [62]. It is more viable for weapons that are produced in bulk, with basic designs that do not require frequent tinkering. Emphasizing more stable, proven weapons over highly technological, risky new systems should increase both reliability and savings. Once past the research and development phase, only about 6% of all contracts are awarded on a competitive basis [63].

Some prime contractors have failed to update outmoded operations. Deputy Secretary of Defense William Taft IV has emphasized that "costly scrap, rework and repair" are frequently caused by the use of obsolescent equipment in manufacturing. "Modernizing factories...will improve control of the manufacturing process and lower total costs...." [64].

Loosening the ties between industry and Pentagon executives [65], the use of unbiased evaluators [66], more rigorous tests [67], greater quality incentives [68], tighter warranties [69], and stricter discipline for shoddy work are all measures that may enhance reliability. Over 1500 contractors have been convicted for fraud; since 1981, more than 1000 have been suspended [70].

In the context of our system of command, control and communication, in the complex warp of the single interaction and reaction system that the Soviet and American arsenals comprise, we cannot afford the luxury of negligence, carelessness, or fraud. While untimely component failure can be the result of *wearout* or of inadequate component design, monitoring, testing, and procurement procedures, even systems with reliable components may prove too complex to work well in crisis conditions. The human factor and the operating environment are predictably subject to malfunction. Strategic defense, launch on warning, short delivery times, and Stealth weapons decrease decision time available, and thereby increase the chance that a false warning generated by a component failure might lead to an automated response.

Finally, components can act in unpredictable ways when placed in complex systems. No matter what level of tolerance is built into the system, an excess of faulty parts may exceed that level. Some systems are too expensive and/or too dangerous to undergo operational testing to discover the unplanned interactions among components, software, the environment, and the human factor.

Is this truly a soluble problem, with so many elements contributing to military component failure?

The honest answer is **no**. As long as the massive stockpiles remain, designed to **deter** but fully ready to be used, governed by fallible command, control and sensing systems and by human response and error, they will be subject to hundreds of thousands of potentially faulty components manufactured *by the lowest bidder*.

But component failure due to short cuts, shoddiness, poor quality control, inadequate design, and failure to respond to specifications can be sharply reduced. In the process, we may anticipate greater reliability and a lessened chance of accidents that may trigger a nuclear exchange in crisis.

References

[1] Perrow, Charles **Normal Accidents: Living with High-Risk Technologies**. (New York: Basic Books, Inc., 1984)

[2] Nakashima, Kyoichi, and Kazuharu Yamato "Variance-importance of system components" in: **I E E E Transactions on Reliability**. Vol. R-31, No. 1, April 1982, pp. 99-100

[3] Jenson, F. and Peterson, N. **Burn-in**. (New York: John Wiley and Sons, 1982) p. 1

[4] Doyle, Edgar A., Jr. "How parts fail" **Reliability: An IEEE Spectrum Compendium**. Oct. 1981, pp. 36-43

[5] Reliability Analysis Center (RAC). **Reliability Design Handbook**. (RDH-376) Rome Air Development Center, Griffith Air Force Base (New York: IIT Research Institute, 1975); Kivenson, Gilbert. **Durability and Reliability in Engineering Design**. (New York: Haydon Book Co., Inc. 1971) pp. 6-8; Doyle, p. 36

[6] RDH, p. 8.

[7] Bernhard, Robert. Lessons from the Military **Reliability: An IEEE Spectrum Compendium**. Oct. 1981, pp. 67-89

[8] RDH, ibid., p. 11; Bernhard, Lessons from the Military

[9] Bernhard, Robert. "Overlooking the obvious" **Reliability: An IEEE Spectrum Compendium** Oct. 1981, p. 85-89

[10] Ibid.

[11] RDH, ibid., p. 171

[12] Ibid., p. 174

[13] Ibid., p. 174-175

[14] Bernhard, Robert "Reliability test procedures," **Reliability: An IEEE Spectrum Compendium** Oct. 1981, pp. 67-68

[15] Lerner, Eric J. "Military electronics: why so unreliabile?" **Aerospace America** Vol. 23, No. 1, Jan. 1985, pp. 106-109

[16] Doyle, ibid., p. 39

[17] Kaplan, Fred "Report: Cruise missile has failed major tests" **Boston Globe**, July 19, 1982

[18] Kaplan, Fred, "Cruise missile 'faulty', says report" **Manchester Guardian,** May 1, 1982

[19] Halloran, Richard "Chief of army assails industry on arms flaws" **The New York Times,** Aug. 9, 1983

[20] Biddle, Wayne. "F-18 builder says test missed design flaws" **The New York Times,** July 28, 1984

[21] Daggett, Stephen. "Dollars and defense: bureaucrats, contractors, and the prospects for reform" **Towson State Journal of International Affairs.** Towson State University, Towson, Maryland. Vol. 20, No. 1, Fall 1985, pp. 9-27. 21

[22] Ibid.

[23] Wallich, Paul. "Today's armies: Plodding toward automation" **IEEE Spectrum.** Oct. 1982, p. 42

[24] Reychav, Uri. **Tolerating the Intolerable: An Engineer's Perspective on Administered Competition in Military Research and Development.** The George Washington University, Engineering Administration Department. 2nd Revised Printing, April, 1989, p. 74; Center for Defense Information (CDI). "Waste in military procurement: The prospects for reform" **The Defense Monitor.** Vol. 15, No. 1, 1986

[25] Daggett, ibid.

[26] "Defect grounds new Army copter" **The New York Times**, Jan. 31, 1986

[27] Gordon, Michael R. "House panel says MX tests indicate serious problems" **The New York Times** August 24, 1987, p. 1

[28] Halloran, Richard "Pentagon tells of key fraud problem" **The New York Times**, October 18, 1987, p. 16

[29] "Faulty control nozzle is suspect in explosion of Trident 2 missile" **The New York Times** March 24, 1989, p. 9

[30] Rosenthal, Andrew "Air force grounds B-1's after a wing punctures a tank" **The New York Times** March 29, 1989, p. 1

[31] Stevenson, Richard W. "Federal indictment says Northrup falsified aerospace test results" **The New York Times** April 12, 1989, p. 1.

[32] Mohr, Charle. "Ex-Pentagon official calls Stealth bomber too costly" **The New York Times** May 20, 1989, p. 8

[33] Christianson, Donald "Reliability" **Reliability: An IEEE Spectrum Compendium** . Oct. 1981, pp. 34-35

[34] McClelland, Lori A. "Mixed review for military semiconducter industry" **Defense Electronics**. Vol. 18, No. 2, Feb. 1986, pp. 39,42,46,49

[35] Hart, Gary, and Barry Goldwater **Report on Recent False Alerts from the Nation's Missile Attack Warning System.** U.S. Senate, Committee on Armed Services. Ninety-sixth Congress. First Session. October 9, 1980. Washington, D.C.: U.S. Government Printing Office, 1980

[36] Doyle, ibid., p. 40

[37] Raines, Marshall L. "Fraud. Guilt. Quiet." **The New York Times**, July 31, 1984

[38] Daggett, Stephen. "Dollars and defense: bureaucrats, contractors, and the prospects for reform.". **Towson State Journal of International Affairs.** Towson State University, Towson, Maryland. Vol. 20, No. 1, Fall 1985, pp. 9-27

[39] Sanger, David E. "Improper microchip testing may bring criminal inquiry" **The New York Times**, Sept. 12, 1984

[40] Ahern, Tim. "Millions of faulty parts for U.S. arms" **Boston Globe,** Sept. 12, 1984

[41] "Testing problem cited at microchip maker" **The New York Times,** Dec. 4, 1984

[42] Lerner, ibid., p. 108

[43] Daggett, ibid., p. 25

[44] CDI, p. 4

[45] Lerner, ibid., p. 106-107

[46] Gumble, Bruce. "Military power supplies getting smaller, tougher." **Defense Electronics.** Vol. 17, No. 4, April 1985, pp. 145-47

[47] Lerner, p. 107; Daggett, pp. 14-55; CDI, p. 4

[48] Daggett, pp. 14,15,19; CDI, p. 4

[49] Taft, William H. Speech given at keynote luncheon for 1985 AFCEA Convention. in: **Signal** Vol. 39, No. 12, Aug. 1985, pp. 25-30

[50] US DOD reliability standardization document program. **IEEE Transactions on Reliability.** Vol. R-28, No. 3, Aug. 1979, pp. 254,258,205

[51] Mason, John F. "A boost for R & M." **Reliability: An IEEE Spectrum Compendium** . Oct. 1981, pp. 76-77

[52] McClelland, ibid., p. 49

[53] Williams, Walter C. "Lessons from NASA" **Reliability: An IEEE Spectrum Compendium** Oct. 1981, pp. 79-84

[54] Lerner, ibid., p. 108

[55] Halloran, 1983, ibid.

[56] RDH, p. 10

[57] Williams, Winston. "Bungling the military buildup" **The New York Times,** January 27, 1985, Sec. 3, p. 1

[58] CDI, p. 7

[59] Daggett, p. 25; Williams, Winston, p. 8

[60] **A Formula for Action.** A report to the president on defense acquisition by the president's blue ribbon commission on defense management. April 25, 1986

[61] Reychav, Tolerating the Intolerable, p. 104

[62] Dagget, p. 26

[63] Williams, ibid.

[64] Taft, pp. 28 & 30

[65] Williams, ibid.

[66] Cushman, John H., Jr. "When weapons don't live up to the specs." **The New York Times,** June 1, 1986, p. E5

[67] Cushman, ibid.

[68] Taft, pp. 25-26

[69] Taft, p. 28; Williams, Walter, p. 8

[70] Taft, ibid.

V. Human Performance Under Stress
A New Scenario for Accidental Nuclear War

Michael D. Wallace

Introduction: Background to Tragedy

At 0654:22 on July 3, 1988 the USS Vincennes, on patrol in the Persian Gulf launched two SM-2 Block II surface-to-air missiles that destroyed a civilian airliner, Iran Air flight 655, with the loss of 290 lives. This tragedy occurred because the captain of the Vincennes, along with the officers and crew in the Combat Information Center (CIC) had come to the mistaken conclusion that Iran Air 655 was an Iranian F-14 fighter about to attack their ship. On the face of it, the error is not easy to explain. When the data tapes of the Vincennes AEGIS system were subsequently analysed, it was discovered that they contained precise and accurate information on the speed, course, position and transponder signal of Iran Air 655, **information which should have identified it unambiguously as a civilian aircraft.**

What then accounts for this appalling mistake? Put simply, it occurred because the Vincennes was not on a training exercise but in combat [1]. The stress of combat affects perception, performance, and judgement in a myriad of subtle and not-so-subtle ways. **Combat stress has an especially potent impact on an individual's ability to evaluate correctly and react appropriately to a complex and rapidly-changing pattern of information.** This fact has profound implications for our ability to prevent a far more hideous accident — this time involving nuclear weapons — in the event of a strategic confrontation.

Some may argue that the present improvement in superpower relations make such a strategic confrontation too remote a prospect for serious concern. But history shows that serious crises and wars often have their origins in events outside the control of the main protagonists. Even in the present climate, an armed rebellion in Eastern Europe or a

73

war between Syria and Israel could rapidly bring the superpowers into serious confrontation, however much they may wish to avoid it. It is worthy of reflection that the crisis leading to World War I erupted at a time when Anglo-German relations were undergoing a marked improvement.

Let us now return to the events of 3 July, 1988, and attempt to account for the Iran Air accident by looking at the events of that morning through the perceptual prism of the officers and crew of the USS Vincennes. On the morning of July 3, the Vincennes, along with the USS Montgomery, observed Iranian gunboats intercepting shipping in the western approaches to the Strait of Hormuz. When the gunboats manoeuvered towards the two ships they opened fire, which the gunboats returned. The forward 5-inch/54-calibre gun (the only weapon available to attack surface targets ahead) malfunctioned. In order to continue firing, the aft 5-inch had to be brought to bear, necessitating a full-rudder turn at 30 knots. While this manoeuver was being executed, shells from the gunboats struck the hull. One can only imagine the tension in the windowless CIC as the deck heeled over at a 30-degree angle and the sounds of machine gun hits rang through the hull. There can be little doubt that this tension contributed substantially to the tragic misperception and error that followed.

The Effects of Combat Stress

In historic times, the stress of combat was a mixture of physical and psychological factors. With contemporary weapons, combat stress is almost entirely psychological. These same weapons also ensure that the pre-combat environment of an acute crisis is almost as stressful as the fighting itself. Combat and crisis create this enormously stressful environment in three ways. First and obviously, it places the individual in extreme physical danger. In the nuclear age, this danger is not confined to front-line troops; every level of command right up to the top political leadership will be acutely aware that their lives hang in the balance during a strategic confrontation.

Second, modern combat and crisis are characterized by acute information overload. As Paul Bracken remarks, "man is by nature a serial processor" (Bracken, 1983, p. 75). When individuals must deal with large numbers of stimuli simultaneously, they will almost certainly ignore, confuse, or misinterpret some of them. The technological advances in modern C^3I systems have multiplied enormously the amount of information available at every level of command. They have not, however, found any way to improve the ability of human beings to cope with it.

Third, modern weapons systems have sharply compressed the time available at all levels of command to make decisions. Much has been written about the effect of compressed decision time in the context of strategic retaliation (Bracken, 1983; Steinbruner, 1984; Wallace, Crissey, & Sennott, 1986) [2]. A major concern of strategic planners and peace activists alike has been that the reduction of effective decision time from hours in the days of the manned bomber to a few minutes in the era of the ICBM sets the stage for an accidental launch if one or both sides believed war was imminent. In the early 1980s, US INF deployments in Europe and Soviet deployment of SSBNs close to North America threatened to reduce effective decision time to zero.

The problem of compressed decision time is even more acute at the tactical level, as the Vincennes incident illustrates so vividly. Only 6 minutes elapsed from first radar contact to missile launch; the airliner was still 17 km. away. **But this was only a few seconds of missile flight time**. So fast-paced has the contemporary tactical environment become that in potential combat situations commanders have no time for sober second thoughts. Their *rules of engagement* tell them to treat any pattern of enemy action which **could** be part of an attack as though it **were** an attack.

Finally, it is critical to understand that these three components of combat stress interact synergistically in a self-enhancing way. Information overload and increased time pressures heighten the individual's anxiety and sense of danger. **Extensive psychological research demonstrates conclusively that heightened anxiety** and sense of danger has a critical impact on an individual's time perception and information processing.

Virtually every researcher has found that threats to life or important values produces a distinct and significant pattern of changes in the decision-making process. Danger induces increased perceptions of time pressure in leaders and commanders, who begin to see their freedom of action as more and more restricted while their adversary's options are perceived to increase (Holsti, 1972; Holsti and George, 1975). They begin to focus on short-term *quick fixes* rather than on the medium or longer term, to concentrate on pre-existing rather than novel information, and to attempt less and less communication with the other side (Janis, 1972). Research in the area of information processing and problem solving has produced quite similar conclusions:

There is agreement that prolonged stress decreases the complexity of information processing. This impairment includes a lessened likelihood of accurately distinguishing between relevant and irrelevant information, reduced search for novel information, the suppression or ignoring of unpleasant inputs, and greater concentration of both incoming and outgoing information to the ingroup. Long-term plans tend to be ignored in favor of stimulus — bound reactions; fine distinctions among items of information or among other participants in the crisis are abandoned, and responses and attitudes become increasingly stereotyped. (Suedfeld and Tetlock, 1977, pp. 170-71)

These findings shape the lethal paradox of contemporary crisis and war; they make superhuman demands on perceptual acuity and decision-making skills, **and those very demands lead to a degrading of both perception and judgement** [3].

Paths to War

In the last few years a great deal of attention has been focussed on the strategic and tactical preconditions of an inadvertent or an accidental nuclear war. Virtually without exception the scenario begins with a major superpower crisis, usually triggered by a new war in the Middle East or a collapse of political order in eastern Europe. This would lead to a major increase in the nuclear alert levels on both sides, creating two major risks. The first is that in the superheated atmosphere of crisis, one side might, through some combination of misinterpretation of the other side's moves, human error, computer glitch, or mechanical malfunction come to believe that an enemy strategic attack was under way. The second risk is that authority to employ battlefield nuclear weapons in the European theatre would be delegated to area commanders, multiplying the number of *fingers on the button* with all its attendant risks.

Although the dangers here are very real, this scenario for an accidental nuclear war is in fact **not** the most probable one. Redeploying tactical nuclear weapons is understood by both sides as exceptionally provocative and would not occur unless a major conventional assault had begun or was about to get underway (Gottfried and Blair, 1988, p. 243). Moreover, it is a strategic *given* for both sides that hostilities would not begin with a strategic attack. Finally, the land-based strategic and tactical systems of both superpowers are equipped with an elaborate set of electronic locks and personnel procedures to prevent launch without National Command Authority authorization (Stein and Feaver, 1987; Meyer, 1987). Thus, unless the conventional forces of both sides are already heavily engaged, or one side took actions that appeared to threaten the strategic C^3I or delivery systems of the other, the accidental or inadvertent use of land-based strategic or tactical systems could probably be avoided at this stage of escalation.

Unfortunately, even if both sides exercise maximum restraint at the strategic nuclear level and do not redeploy tactical nuclear weapons in Europe, there remains one arena in which a relatively low level of nuclear alert would quickly set in motion a train of events in which a tactical miscalculation or accident very low in the chain of command could result in the loss of conventional assets deemed vital, a serious threat to strategic forces, or even the breaching of the nuclear threshold. Needless to say, any of these events would

77

represent a major escalation of the conflict with potentially disastrous consequences. At a minimum, they would result in additional alerting measures, increasing enormously the risk of an accidental strategic launch. Such events could themselves be misinterpreted as the beginning of a strategic attack, inducing one or both sides to pre-empt. They would multiply the inevitable uncertainties of the *fog of war*. And finally, they would almost certainly lead to further escalation and loss of control at the tactical level, dragging the antagonists down the slippery slope to Armageddon. This nightmare scenario would begin unseen beneath the surface of the world's oceans.

Submarine Warfare: High Stakes, High Risks

The danger that World War III might begin as the result of submarine actions arises from the interaction of four factors: the critical role ballistic missile firing submarines play in the strategic deterrent of both sides; the strategic doctrine governing the mission and tactics of superpower naval forces, especially on the American side; the uniquely uncertain and dangerous tactical environment of submarine warfare; and the near impossibility of maintaining communications with and control over submerged submarines under combat or crisis conditions.

Since the 1960s the ballistic missile firing submarine has played a critical role as the third leg of the US strategic triad. Untrackable in the deep oceans, the mission of the US SSBN force has always been to provide the ability to ride out a Soviet nuclear attack and thus provide a certain retaliatory capability. With the deployment of the Navstar satellite positioning system and the Trident II D-5 missile about to be deployed in American Ohio-class ships, the American SSBN fleet will be capable of counterforce targetting against Soviet land-based missile silos as well (Feiveson and Duffield, 1988). Assuming D-5 deployments go ahead as planned and that no additional MX missiles are deployed, a substantial majority of US strategic warheads will be at sea by the mid-1990s.

Geography and technological inferiority have traditionally relegated the SSBN to a position of inferiority among Soviet strategic nuclear forces. But with the deployment of MX and D5 representing a serious threat to their silo-based ICBM force, in the 1980s the Soviets began to place more emphasis on their submarine fleet. The very quiet Delta-IV ships with their long range SS-N-23 missiles are now on station in the Sea of Okhotsk bastion, while the huge new double-hulled Typhoon SSBNs with their solid-fuel SS-N-20 missiles are on station under the ice in the Barents Sea (Handler and Arkin, 1988; MccGwire, 1988). Further evidence of the importance the Soviets attach to the security of their SSBN forces may be found in the number of attack submarines (SSNs) and surface ships and planes dedicated to their protection (Stefanick, 1986, p. 13).

It is in the light of this critical Soviet interest that we must evaluate US naval strategy as it has developed since 1982. In that year, Secretary of the Navy Lehmann and Chief of Naval Operations Watkins announced a new mission for the Navy in the event of hostilities with the Soviet Union: to attack Soviet SSBNs and their bases in and around their bastions in the Barents Sea and Sea of Okhotsk. To do this, carrier battle groups and American attack submarines would be placed on station for such an attack at a fairly early stage in a crisis (Mearsheimer, 1988). In other words, at the first stage of strategic alert — DEFCON 3 — American naval forces would be manoeuvering close to Soviet submarines and their bases, so as to be in a position to attack them at a moment's notice if ordered.

The Soviets are clearly alarmed by this strategy. They have responded to the large American fleet exercises designed to practice these manoeuvers by engaging in confrontational tactics with American ships and submarines, and these have resulted in collisions, aggressive aerial counterpatrolling down the west coast of North America, and Soviet air alerts (Wallace and Meconis, 1988) [4]. It is widely believed that one such alert in 1983 helped set the stage for the shootdown of KAL 007 (Hersh, 1985). Nor should it be thought that the US has abandoned this strategy in the light of improving superpower relations; another large fleet exercise of this type (codenamed PacEx89) is scheduled for the fall of 1989.

If mere exercises have nearly brought the superpowers to blows, one can only imagine the perils of an actual confrontation in the terrifying environment of a nuclear alert. This is particularly true in the undersea environment, where the perils are greater and the difficulties in acquiring reliable tactical information are almost without parallel. To begin with, submarine warfare is always *for keeps*. If a land target or surface ship is hit with a conventional weapon, there is at least some probability of personal survival. On board a submarine, serious damage means almost certain death. Moreover, underwater the hunters are always the hunted as well. Even modern and very sophisticated submarines could fall victim to their intended targets, since the very actions and manoeuvers used to detect and track enemies may cause them to be detected and tracked in turn (Compton-Hall, 1987).

The battle environment of the submarine is quite literally opaque to its commander and officers. For the most part, a submarine closely engaged with the enemy must rely almost entirely on its passive sonar (acoustaphones) for tactical information. Any other source of information (active sonar, periscope, or towed radio antenna) increases the chance of detection. At the best of times passive sonar provides somewhat ambiguous information about the identity, location, and speed of an object. In waters characterized by thermal and salinity layering which distort underwater sound (such as the Arctic or Mediterranean) the ambiguity may be nearly total (Sakitt, 1987). On at least one occasion, a NATO submarine commander almost attacked a fishing fleet when acoustic distortion led him to believe it was a Soviet submarine pack about to attack. Even under the best of acoustic conditions, there are many tactical situations in which defensive measures taken by one submarine might sound like offensive measures to another. For example, the deployment of acoustic decoys to shake off another submarine may sound to the opponent like a torpedo attack.

The complexity of a modern submarine multiplies the confusion: "There are vastly more dials and digits in the attack centre of a submarine today and it is not unknown for them to hypnotize a commanding officer, misleading judgement and common sense." (Moore and Compton-Hall, 1987, p. 83).

Thus it is clear that in submarine combat, the chances of miscalculation and accident are extremely high, certainly higher than in surface combat. If the effect of combat stress was potent in the Vincennes, it would likely be more so on board submarines in close contact with one another during a crisis. In these circumstances, it would be only a matter of time before some submarine commander somewhere mistakenly believed himself to be under attack and launched his own attack in self-defence.

All of this is further aggravated by the difficulties in communicating with submarines. Submerged and in action, a submarine can receive only agonizingly slow low-frequency messages and cannot transmit at all. Only by trailing a visible and noisy antenna (and putting his vessel at risk) can a commander send and receive tactical information from headquarters or other forces. For that reason, he will probably be largely ignorant of military and political developments, and in turn headquarters may be ignorant of his fate [5].

Thus, once the crisis begins, command authority will lose virtually all communication with, and control over, the undersea battle. Alone, vulnerable, and with a limited and probably inaccurate view of the strategic and tactical picture, the submarine commander and his crew will have to make decisions that may affect the fate of the planet.

How the Undersea Battle Could Escalate

Once American and Soviet submarines begin to confront each other, disaster could happen in a number of ways. One danger is that Soviet authorities might come to believe that a large part of their SSBN force has been or is about to be destroyed. They would of course expect to lose some vessels, but major, sudden losses might lead them to believe that the US anti-SSBN attacks are the prelude to a pre-emptive strike on their land-based missiles. In that case, a pre-emptive attack of their own might appear to be the most attractive option; it would allow them to use at least some of their SLBMs in the attack and would disrupt American C^3I sufficiently to lessen damage to the Soviet Union.

Faced with this scenario, advocates of the Maritime Strategy have argued for a gradual, controlled attack on Soviet SSBNs (Pocalyko, 1987). But a North American authority on submarine warfare argues that this is unrealistic:

... the course of the undersea battle would appear vague and confusing to leaders on both sides. An anti-SSBN campaign would be fought largely by attack submarines **operating independently** in Soviet waters. Conditions for two-way communications would be poor. Even if given the order to withdraw ... US submarines would most likely have to fight their way out, and any mines placed by the US SSNs would continue to threaten Soviet vessels. In the extremely hostile environment, attack subs could ill afford the time to distinguish between different types of Soviet submarines. Both sides would realize that, **once set in motion, a submarine campaign could not be "fine tuned" reliably in an attempt to make it less provocative** (Stefanick, 1986) [6].

Even if Soviet command refrained from giving an order to fire, there is still the chance that one or more Soviet SSBNs might fire their missiles independently if they came to believe that a strategic exchange had already begun. Although control over Soviet strategic weapons is extremely centralized, it appears that an independent launch could be made if there were agreement between the ship's sailing officers, the Strategic Rocket Forces (RVSN) personnel in charge of the missiles, and the political officer (*Zampolit*) (Meyer, 1987, p. 492). If they had been cut off from communications with headquarters for some time, had heard the sounds of other Soviet submarines being destroyed, were under direct attack themselves, and especially if they had heard the detonation of a tactical nuclear weapon, these officers might indeed believe that World War III had already begun and that their duty was to complete their mission before being destroyed.

This scenario dovetails with another: that, seeing its submarines rapidly being destroyed, Soviet authorities would authorize the use of tactical nuclear weapons against attacking American forces. This would be a tempting option, as it would postpone a strategic exchange, while at the same time seizing the tactical advantage: "If and when the nuclear threshold is crossed, the advantage shifts almost decisively to the Soviet Navy" (Parker, 1982, p. 5). The US has attempted to rule out this option by its stated threat to respond to a Soviet use of tactical weapons at sea with a nuclear attack on Soviet naval bases. But since such an attack would in fact amount to the initiation of a strategic exchange, it is difficult to see the threat as credible. Recently, even proponents of the Maritime Strategy have begun to worry about its escalatory implications: "... military staffs need to assess the impact of non-nuclear actions on vertical escalation. **We must make a concerted effort not to blunder into nuclear war**" (Tritten, 1987, p. 66).

A final risk is that an **American** submarine would use a tactical nuclear weapon if its officers believed it necessary in self-defense. It is more than likely that in a crisis surface forces and submarines alike would have pre-delegated authority to use nuclear weapons in certain specific circumstances, for example if preparations for a Soviet tactical nuclear attack were detected (Bracken, 1983, p. 366). Under the stress of combat and in the murky submerged environment, even the discipline, cool professionalism, and rigorous training of US submarine crews might not prevent the launch of a tactical nuclear weapon in the mistaken belief that a Soviet attack was under way; in other words, an underwater, nuclear Vincennes incident.

The risk is compounded by the fact that despite careful screening, inevitably some personnel will exhibit substandard performance or even manifest psychological abnormalities [7]. In one case, a NATO submarine was commanded by an officer later discovered to suffer from paranoid delusions. While at sea, he became obsessed with the idea that his submarine was being tracked by a Soviet ship and managed to convince his officers and crew that this phantom was real.

Eventually, to avoid his imaginary pursuer, he grounded his submarine in shallow water. One can only imagine the result if this officer were to be in command during a major US-Soviet submarine engagement.

It would appear, then, that the risk of an accidental nuclear war beginning as the result of submarine action at a relatively low level of escalation is extremely serious. Yet, it has received relatively little attention from either the media or the policy community, especially in comparison with the enormous amount of attention focussed on the land theatre in Europe. This is all the more surprising given the importance of naval forces to US policy goals virtually everywhere in the world. In every theatre **other** than in Central Europe, the first superpower forces to confront each other in a crisis would be naval ones. It is perhaps not inappropriate to note in this context that of the seven major wars the US has fought, five have begun with naval engagements.

Arms Control at Sea: A Pressing Need

There have been several substantial arms control proposals put forward to reduce this risk of the early escalation of submarine warfare [8]. Understandably, the Soviet Union has taken the initiative in this area. They have proposed that zones in the Pacific be designated as sanctuaries in which ASW activities would be prohibited and that large naval exercises near populated coasts be restricted (Purver, 1988). Such proposals have been rejected by American officials, who argue that they would represent a unilateral concession by the US and that they would free Soviet SSNs now protecting the Soviet SSBN bastions to attack western sea lines of communication in both the Atlantic and the Pacific.

Many Western arms control experts argue that this summary rejection may not in fact be in the best interests of the US or of the West as a whole (Hill, 1989; Mack, 1988; Meconis, 1989; Purver, 1988). In addition to the risk of accidental war detailed above, a combination of technological developments and the constraints imposed by the tentative strategic weapons ceilings agreed to at the START talks will create powerful pressures for the negotiation of a superpower naval arms control agreement.

First, it is evident that the START ceilings on strategic nuclear warheads cannot be achieved without at least some reduction in the number of SSBNs possessed by each side. This necessity is strengthened by the SSBN modernization programs of both sides, which are seeing the replacement of smaller submarines with larger ones carrying more launch tubes. In effect, both sides will be placing more eggs in a smaller number of baskets, a situation which may begin to undermine the confidence of both sides in the security of their sea-based deterrent.

It is important to stress that this vulnerability is no longer asymmetrical; a second development, the shrinking of the *acoustic gap* between Soviet and American SSNs, may for the first time lead to questions about the security of the American SSBN fleet. Although this threat is still a distance away, Western strategic planners can hardly be encouraged by a situation in which fewer and fewer SSBNs are pursued by ever more, ever quieter and more sophisticated Soviet SSNs.

An additional pressure is created by the development of a new generation of land-attack submarine-launched cruise missiles. From the outset, US negotiators have resisted the inclusion of SLCMs in a new START agreement. The US side believes that it enjoys a substantial lead in this technology, and that limiting SLCMs would entail insurmountable verification problems (Mack, 1988, p. 12). But the rapid pace with which the Soviets are closing the gap combines with geography to create a formidable threat to the US and Europe. The new Soviet SS-NX-24 cruise missile, which may have both supersonic and stealth capabilities, will no doubt be deployed soon in the absence of a superpower agreement (Mack, 1988, p. 13). The US and Europe stand to lose in an SLCM race, since far more of their population, industry, and strategic assets are within SLCM range than is the case with the Soviet Union. The disadvantage is compounded by the Soviets' considerably larger number of attack submarines that could be converted to SLCM platforms (Handler and Arkin, 1988, pp. 21-22).

85

In short, American resistance to naval arms control is becoming increasingly untenable. It is vital that naval forces begin to receive the same attention in superpower relations that has already been accorded strategic nuclear forces and European conventional forces.

Naval Arms Control : Some Policy Proposals

There are three types of superpower agreements that could go a long way to alleviate these risks and threats. In the short term it would be possible to negotiate quickly a series of confidence-building measures that would defuse the tensions created by the Maritime Strategy. These might range from such simple steps as pre-notification of naval exercises and exchange of observers to strengthening the Prevention of Incidents at Sea Agreement by including a formula specifying minimum distances of approach (Meconis, 1989). More far-reaching CBMs would incorporate the Soviet notion of ASW exclusion zones, perhaps in tandem with an SSBN exclusion zone near the American coasts as a quid pro quo (Purver, 1988, p. 13). Although questions of verifiability have been raised, the consensus in the strategic community is that these are not overwhelming obstacles (Purver, 1988 pp. 14-18).

In the medium term CBMs could be supplemented by arms control measures restricting nuclear SLCMs. The Soviet Union has proposed a ceiling of 400 for each side, with a ban on their deployment on surface ships. The US side has raised serious concerns about the verifiability of such restrictions, and in particular the difficulty of distinguishing between nuclear and non-nuclear cruise missiles. However, many arms control experts believe that schemes for random inspection and tagging of shipborne missiles could be devised that would satisfy reasonable verification concerns (Tsipis, 1988). It is worthy of note that a total ban of SLCMs would be easier to verify than quantitative restrictions.

A final proposal would see deep cuts in the number of nuclear attack submarines permitted on each side. Such a disarmament agreement would be extremely easy to verify and would have a number of extremely important advantages

(Meconis, 1989, pp. 11-13). First, reducing the number of SSNs would greatly help the task of verifying restrictions or bans on SLCMs. Second, a smaller number of SSNs would lessen the threat to the smaller, post-START SSBN fleet. Third, cutting SSN numbers would alleviate Western concerns about the Soviet threat to their SLOCs. Fourth, since the Soviets currently have twice the number of SSNs possessed by the US, deep asymmetrical cuts to an identical agreed ceiling would probably garner considerable support in the US. Fifth, since nuclear submarines are among the most costly of all weapons systems, a halt in SSN procurement would provide great savings for both sides; this fiscal incentive could prove politically powerful [9]. Finally, and most important of all, fewer SSNs would greatly reduce the risk that submarine actions during a crisis would lead to an accidental war in the manner detailed above.

To sum up: justifiable concern with the risk of accidental nuclear war originating from developments in the strategic, INF, and European theatre arms races has led western strategists to overlook the risk of an accidental war as a product of the arms race at sea. This omission must be remedied by more research into naval arms control. At the policy level, the US and other NATO countries should take up Gorbachev's invitation to begin talks on naval disarmament measures.

Notes

[1] Note that the Commanding Officer of the USS Sides (which was **not** involved in action at that time) correctly concluded that the unknown aircraft was probably an Iranian airliner, even though the radar system on board the Sides was far less powerful and sophisticated than the Vincennes' AEGIS system. (Department of Defense, 1988, P.E-62 & E-66); Carter (1989).

[2] It has been argued that one reason for the cautious and measured approach of the US leadership group during the Cuban Missile Crisis was their perception at the beginning of the crisis that they had several days to seek

out new intelligence and weigh alternatives (Gottfried and Blair, 1988, p. 264).

[3] Of course, there are those rare individuals who seem almost immune from the stress of crisis or combat (Gottfried and Blair, 1988, p. 266; Wallace and Suedfeld, 1988). But in both the political and military realms they are certainly outnumbered by those whose unresolved inner conflicts and/or unhappy interpersonal relationships make them even more vulnerable to stress, as noted below.

[4] It might be supposed that the 1972 Agreement on the Prevention of Incidents on and over the High Seas would lessen the risks of such confrontations (Lynn-Jones, 1985). While this treaty has reduced the annual number of such incidents from 100 to 40, the lack of a *safe distance* rule makes it ineffective in many situations (Wallace and Meconis, 1988, p. 33). Moreover, underwater operations are specifically exempt. In any case, in a major crisis the Agreement would probably be a dead letter.

[5] In the DEFCON 3 alert during the 1973 Yom Kippur war, US and Soviet submarine forces remained engaged for several days after the crisis had ended. (Gottfried and Blair, 1988, pp. 202-03).

[6] Many submarine officers have attested to the confusing effect of minelaying on submarine operations. See Patton (1988).

[7] One analyst of submarine combat operations claims that only 6% of peacetime submarine commanders prove effective in combat. (Carver, 1989).

[8] An excellent compendium of naval arms control proposals was put together by the Department of Disarmament Affairs of the United Nations in 1986. (See bibliography.)

[9] It is widely assumed that fiscal considerations were behind the Canadian government's decision early in 1989 to cancel its proposed purchase of 10-12 SSNs.

Bibiliography

Bracken, P. **The Command and Control of Nuclear Forces** (New Haven: Yale University Press, 1983)

Carter, E.W. "Friend or Foe?" **US Naval Institute Proceedings,** (1989) v.115/5, pp. 78-80

Carver, C.J. A letter in **US Naval Institute Proceedings** (1989) v.115/6, pp. 24-28

Compton-Hall, R. **Submarine versus Submarine: The Tactics and Technology of Underwater Confrontation** (New York: Orion Books, 1988)

Department of Defense. **Investigation Report: Formal Investigation into the Circumstances Surrounding the Downing of Iran Air Flight 655 on 3 July 1988** (Washington: US Department of Defense, 1988)

Feiveson, H.A., and Duffield, J. "Stopping the Sea-Based Counterforce Threat" in: **Naval Strategy and National Security** Steven E. Miller and Stephen Van Evera, eds., (Princeton: Princeton Unversity Press, 1988)

Friedman, N. "The Vincennes Incident" **US Naval Institute Proceedings** (1989) Vol. 115/5, pp. 72-9

Gottfried, K., and Blair, B. **Crisis Stability and Nuclear War** (New York: Oxford University Press, 1989)

Handler, J., and Arkin, W. M. **Nuclear Warships and Naval Nuclear Weapons: A Complete Inventory** Neptune Papers no. 2 (Washington: Institute for Policy Studies, 1988)

Hersh, S.M. **The Target is Destroyed: What Really Happened to Flight 007 and What America Knew About It** (New York: Random House, 1985)

Hill, J.R. **Arms Control at Sea.** (Annapolis: Naval Institute Press, 1989)

Holsti, O.R. **Crisis, Escalation and War** (Montréal: McGill-Queens University Press, 1972)

Holsti, O.R., and George, A.L. "The Effects of Stress on the Performance of Foreign Policy Makers" in: **Political Science Annual: An International Review** C.P. Cotter ed. (Indianapolis: Bobbs-Merrill, 1975) p. 255-319

Janis, I.L. **Victims of Groupthink** (Boston: Houghton Mifflin, 1972)

Mack, A. **Arms Control in the North Pacific** Working Paper no.36 of the Peace Research Centre (Canberra: Australian National University, 1988)

MccGwire, M. **Military Objectives in Soviet Foreign Policy** (Washington: Brookings, 1987)

Mearsheimer, J.J. "A Strategic Misstep: The Maritime Strategy and Deterrence in Europe" in Miller and Van Evera, op.cit.

Meconis, C.A. **A Non-provocative Navy for the Nineties** Working Paper no.4. (Seattle: Institute for Global Security Studies, 1989)

Meyer, S.M. "Soviet Nuclear Operations" in: **Managing Nuclear Operations.**Carter, A.B., Steinbruner, J.D., and Zracket, C.A., eds. (Washington: Brookings, 1987) pp. 470-531

Moore, J.E., and Compton-Hall, R. **Submarine Warfare Today and Tomorrow** (Bethesda, Maryland: Adler & Adler, 1987)

Parker, T.W. "Theatre Nuclear Warfare and the US Navy", **Naval War College Review,** January-February 1982, pp. 2-7

Patton, J.H. "ASW: Winning the Race" **US Naval Institute Proceedings,** 1988, Vol. 114/6, pp. 64-66

Pocalyko, M.N. "Sinking Soviet SSBNs" **US Naval Institute Proceedings,** October, 1987, pp. 26-36

Purver, R.G. **SSBN Sanctuaries for Submarine Stand-off Zones: A Possible Naval Arms Control Tradeoff** Paper prepared for the 52nd Pugwash Symposium on 'Naval Forces: Arms Restraint and Confidence Building', Oslo, Norway, 23-26 June, 1988

Sakitt, M. **Submarine Warfare in the Arctic: Option or Illusion?** An Occasional Paper of the Center for International Security and Arms Control. (Stanford: Stanford University Press, 1988)

Stefanick, T.A. "America's Maritime Strategy: The Arms Control Implications" **Arms Control Today** December, 1986, pp. 10-17

Stein, P., and Feaver, P. **Assuring Control of Nuclear Weapons: The Evolution of Permissive Action Links** Occasional Paper No. 2 of the Center for Science and International Affairs, Harvard University (Boston: University Press of America, 1987)

Steinbruner, J.D. "Launch Under Attack" **Scientific American** Vol. 250 No. 3, 1984. pp. 33-41

Suedfeld, P., and Tetlock, P.E. "Integrative Complexity of Communications in International Crises" **Journal of Conflict Resolution**, 1977 Vol. 21 No. 1 pp. 169-84

Tritten, J.J. "Nonnuclear Escalation" **US Naval Institute Proceedings**, February, 1987, pp. 61-8

Tsipis, K. "Arms Control Verification at Sea: Cruise Missiles," **Naval Forces**, 1988. Vol. 9 No. 3, pp. 42-52

United Nations **The Naval Arms Race** Study Series 16, 1986, Department of Disarmament Affairs

Wallace, M.D., Crissey, B.L., and Sennott, L.I. "Accidental Nuclear War: A Risk Assessment," **Journal of Peace Research**, 1986, Vol. 23 No. 1, pp. 9-27

Wallace, M.D., and Meconis, C.A., **Superpower Naval Rivalry and Command Survivability** Paper presented to the conference on Maritime Security and Arms Control in the Pacific Region. (Vancouver, Canada: University of British Columbia, 1988)

Wallace, M.D., and Suedfeld, P. "Leadership Performance in Crisis: The Longevity - Complexity Link" **International Studies Quarterly**, 1988 Vol. 32 No. 4, p. 439-51

VI. Accidental Nuclear War in Europe

Horst Afheldt

While the probability of unintended **strategic** nuclear war is generally low, this is not the case for unintended nuclear war in Europe. This is because NATO's strategy for the defense of Europe, the strategy of flexible response, is based on **deliberate** nuclear escalation. On behalf of deterrence, NATO, therefore, is obliged to keep the probability of nuclear escalation (following the onset of a conventional war) rather high. Consequently, war in Europe, intended or not, would bring with it the very real danger of nuclear war.

This NATO strategy is defined in three stages:

First stage: Direct defense without the use of nuclear weapons in the first instance, but with the possibility of using nuclear weapons at any time should their use be deemed necessary.

Second stage: Deliberate escalation with nuclear weapons.

Third stage: All-out nuclear war.

The deliberate nuclear escalation (stage two) is supposed to convince the aggressor to retreat and to accept peace under conditions favorable to NATO. If ever applied, that artifact may or may not work. Nothing can be proven in advance. Therefore, NATO's strategy bases the fate of the European continent on a desire and a conviction about complicated military preparations that can never be tested. Yet all experience with military action in history shows that most things will go wrong. For Europeans, it seems like *American optimism* to base the fate of a continent on a hope that is set against all experience.

This optimism is no longer shared in Central Europe. Eighty percent of the young population reject a security policy based on the threat of a first use of nuclear weapons. The former Chancellor Schmidt declared that should nuclear weapons be used in Europe, the German Army would

92

surrender.   Chancellor Kohl called back the German participants in NATO's last exercise, WINTEX, when its planners started to include the simulated use of nuclear weapons.

This is not the place to detail the complicated interplay between conventional defense and nuclear deterrence. It is sufficient to state that, the more reliable conventional defense becomes, the lower the likelihood of nuclear first use will be. The more reliable the conventional defense, the higher the chance of avoiding unintended nuclear escalation, preplanned in the NATO strategy. Given the element of preplanning in the NATO strategy, I call such a nuclear war an **incidental** nuclear war.

The first approach to reducing the possibility of incidental nuclear war was NATO's repeated demand to balance the vast superiority of conventional Warsaw Pact forces with an **arms build-up**. That attempt, however, contributed to the arms race and fell short of the desired success.   The second approach is the current attempt, to reduce the forces of both sides in Europe to equal levels by **disarmament**. The Vienna disarmament talks, with this objective in mind, may or may not be successful. Let's suppose they are successful. Will the military situation in Europe be stable in this event? Will there remain no danger of that unintended but preplanned nuclear escalation?

In April 1940 the Wehrmacht attacked France with thirty percent fewer tanks and about half the number of fighter planes the Allies could muster. The attack was successful because of its particular offensive strategy. In 1941 the Wehrmacht attacked the Soviet Union with an inferiority ranging from 1:3 to 1:12, depending on the weapon systems, and was again initially successful for the same reason.

The present West German army was built up using the ideas which were developed in the 1930s **for an optimal offensive strategy**. All armies in Europe are children of the old Wehrmacht. The ideal offensive army is a fully motorized one. Only twenty percent of Hitler's army in 1940 were tank divisions; the rest were on foot. The Bundeswehr of today is a hundred percent Panzer and Panzergrenadier divisions, which is Guderian's ideal for offense. That means that initiative and attack are more favored by today's army than they were in 1940 and 1941. Thus, the Air Land Battle Doctrine of the US Army of today states quite rightly that initiative and attack allow a small army to defeat a stronger one.

But if that is right, then even after the disarmament of the Warsaw Pact Forces to an equilibrium in Europe, a conventional battle in a future war in Europe would very likely be won by the side that **started** the war. Whoever does **not** desire to start a war and follows the defensive policy never to shoot first has lost the war from the very beginning. NATO has such a no-first-shoot policy.

The reaction of NATO to this dilemma is a political ballet. After years of pretending that the only reason for nuclear weapons on the battlefield in Europe is the vast superiority of the Warsaw Pact's conventional forces, NATO is now starting to say that even if there should one day be equal levels of conventional forces on both sides in Europe, no denuclearization of Europe could be accepted.

In addition, there is another problem. The modern armies in Europe are based upon an intelligent combination of tactics and strategy for rapidly overcoming and defeating a powerful defense. One basic element for offense is the combination of air force and tanks. For a defender who developed and trained such an army, optimized for attack, with the unhappy mission to **defend** with that army, the air force remains a basic element. This fact was very clearly revealed in the Normandy battle in 1944. The defending German army which had lost practically all its air strength could consequently bring no tank division to the battle in time. Today, NATO is as dependent on air strength for its defense with mechanized divisions as the Germans were in 1944. But today's NATO air forces are based on a limited number of airfields.

NATO countries are currently developing missiles that are capable of destroying not only airfields, but also most airplanes in hangers at distances of up to 500 km. This system was developed by Bölkow and Martin Marietta. It is quite certain that not only NATO will have this capability in the years to come, but the Warsaw Pact will as well. So, even if both sides reduce their conventional forces to equal numbers, we will have a situation in Europe where the side who is waiting for a crisis always knows that if their adversary should fire these missiles against their airfields and destroy their remaining airplanes in a subsequent air attack, he has nearly won the conventional battle. It would not be an overstatement to say that the attacked side either would have to capitulate or to use nuclear weapons immediately. So the probability of preplanned but unintended nuclear escalation persists.

It is clear that NATO's old claim of equal levels for the opposing forces in Europe could not solve the dilemma of unintended but preplanned nuclear escalation, which is the problem of incidental nuclear war in Europe.

It was possible to anticipate that scenario 10 or 15 years ago. It was clear that a new conventional strategy was needed and had to be elaborated. The new strategy demanded a new army-structure, optimized for **defense**, to comply with criteria inverse to the rules for the existing armies, which are optimized for offense. An army optimized for defense further needed a new specialized conventional tactic and new rules for the development of specialized conventional arms. This was not an easy task. It was done by the same kind of re-examination of fundamentals which de Gaulle, Liddell Hart, Fuller, Guderian and others had been forced to pursue.

The goal of mutual defensive-superiority will be accomplished when the chances for an attacker to succeed are twenty percent or less and the probability of successful defense becomes eighty percent or more. If that objective could be attained, then, in case of war, the temptation or necessity to go nuclear, would be reduced drastically. Also the probability of any attack would be greatly reduced — war prevention by denial.

The theoretical part of the work developing defensive strategies has now been done and the results have been presented, for example, in the Pugwash Working Group on

Conventional Forces in Europe. Here I only reiterate the principles:

The first principle is stability in peace.

This means that both sides are deterred from attacking with the knowledge that the chances of succeeding in an attack are extremely low, and that, in all likelihood, the defense will triumph.

Stability in peace also requires armaments that pose little or no threat to the other side, nor create an inclination to start an arms race.

The second principle is stability in crises.

Stability in crises demands, above all, that defense does not depend on focal points which can be destroyed by the adversary in a surprise attack. Today, that necessitates, above all, that NATO and WTO no longer depend on air strength for their defense. This principle of crisis stability is the most important criterion for a no-first-shoot army. And such an army is the only army which fits the declared NATO policy, i.e. the defensive policy.

The third principle is stability in war against unintended escalation.

This means a reliable conventional defense. And this can only be achieved by the defender's superiority over the offense.

Most of the work designing such a strategy of defensive superiority was done in Central Europe by soldiers and civilian researchers outside the defense departments. Not enough work, however, has been done inside the framework of those departments. I can't judge what has happened in this context in the United States nor what has happened in the Soviet Union; but I can see that the present Soviet proposals for the reduction and the restructuring of conventional forces in Europe show more regard for those basic questions of structure, strategy and doctrines than NATO statements do.

Now it is time for NATO to start the difficult and challenging work of restructuring and optimizing NATO forces for defense only. Success or failure in this effort bears directly upon the basic problems of unintended nuclear war and nuclear escalation which are inherent in NATO strategy.

VII. The Kaleidoscope of International Decision Making
Glimpsing the Human Factors in Nuclear Crisis

Rita R. Rogers

"Preventive war is like suicide from fear of death."
Otto von Bismarck

There are many factors, issues, and influences which ultimately coalesce into the threatening possibility of accidental nuclear war. Here we will explore the human factors which could lead to an international crisis and hence to a nuclear disaster.

The decision-making process is a volatile arena in which international crises can be all too easily precipitated. Decision making in international relations is profoundly affected by the emotional climate in which it is occurring. This emotional climate is a product of cultural, social, economic, and political factors, together with the personality characteristics of the decision-maker and the relationships within the decision-making team. Over three decades ago, Harold Nicholson vividly described the texture and composition of this emotional climate [1]:

The structure of any international crisis is organic rather than artificial. It is the result of gradual growth, and however much one may seek to detach and mount the specimens for purposes of exposition, it must never be forgotten that at the time, *they were part of the thought, feeling, and action of sentient beings, exposed to all the impulses and fallibility of human nature.* [Italics added]

Cultural Factors

The "thought, feeling, and action of sentient beings" is very much shaped by the culture in which they live. (*Culture* is defined as a "pretested design, socially created, tested,

97

shared, learned and internalized" [2]). The cultural lens through which a decision-maker and his team perceives or misperceives a threat is influenced by the **collective memory** [3] they share. Collective memory is transmitted from generation to generation and determines some of the mindsets which have an important impact on the decision-making process.

For example, the concept of *nuclear deterrence* is derived from an assumption that is rooted in psychological dynamics: that the threat of devastating destruction will be perceived by the *other side* as reason to resist its fermenting inclination to start a war [4]. Yet, perceptions of what constitutes a threat differ from country to country and from culture to culture. Each culture will perceive events/actions differently, through the prism of its unique collective memory. In a crisis the psychological determinants of a preemptive attack will vary from culture to culture. In order to evaluate accurately the way in which an action taken by one culture will be viewed by another culture, there is a tremendous need for cultural and political exchange and the expanded awareness such an exchange can generate.

The Decision-maker

The bio/psycho/social complex which comprises the personality of the decision-maker will have a profound impact on the decision-making process. The decision-maker's image of himself as a caretaker or as a catalyst, his tendency to procrastinate or initiate, his blend of patriotism, political ambitions, and humanistic sensibilities will all be important ingredients in his decision-making process. A nuclear crisis demands from the decision-maker an ability to rethink and re-evaluate old concepts, which in turn requires a solid sense of security in both his personal and national identities. This psychological security then permits the recognition and acceptance of the fact that the *adversary* also sees himself as a patriot.

This process of review and re-evaluation cannot be accomplished when the decision-maker does not accept the parameters of the political, legal, and structural responsibilities of his office. Under such circumstances, a decision-maker is more likely to delegate to subordinates the decision-making tasks which should remain in his sole domain. He avoids confronting his own limitations by ordering others to do what he should do — thus maintaining an illusion of unlimited power. It is this struggle between passivity and aggressiveness, together with a feeling of uneasy dependency, which can elicit a fierce need to assume a compensatory exhibitionistic stance of independence. This kind of posturing can lead to premature or ill-considered actions, with disastrous consequences.

In today's technological world, we also need to include the decision-maker's ability to project and convey his conviction, determination, motivation, and commitment via the media. The decision-maker's support base will be shaped by his own self-image, by what he perceives to be his nation's role in the world, and by the expectations of his constituency. In the US, promises made to the electorate create a particular climate in which later decisions are made. For example, President Kennedy's inaugural address was imbued with a missionary zeal which influenced his initial tone and approach to the Cuban missile crisis [5].

In the case of nuclear crisis, if the decision-maker misperceives his electorate's expectations of him, his ability to command, control, and communicate might be severely hindered. In an interesting article, Miroslav Nincic [6], reports that the US election of a "hawkish" president ironically wants him to be accommodating, while a "dovish" president is expected to take a "strong stance".

In a crisis, a preceding molding event often has a profound impact on the decision-maker's perspective and this internalized event becomes a lens through which the decision-maker sees the present. The decision-maker will be more inclined to judge from the perspective of the past when he is facing a completely unknown and unimaginable situation. In addition, the constraints of time limitations and stress levels will provide a strong impetus to view the present from the perspective of the past. This is even more likely to occur when the decision-maker feels guilty or ambivalent about his past decision-making abilities. He might be determined *not to make another mistake*. The degree to which the decision-maker can deal with negative outcomes depends primarily on his sense of selfhood and self-esteem.

Individuals vary in their cognitive and emotional abilities to process information. The capacity to perceive and decipher prodromal signs of a crisis demands open-mindedness, courage, flexibility, and trust in one's *instincts* and intuitions. Other personality characteristics — such as tendencies toward the use of denial and scapegoating, excessive rationalization or rumination, and unresolved rivalries — all will have an impact on the decision-maker in times of crisis.

Beyond these personality proclivities that fall within the normal range of accepted behavior, we also need to consider the possibility that a leader may be seriously incapacitated due to psychotic illness. When that is the case, there is a pervasive impairment of judgment, faulty reality testing, and an inability to control impulsive behavior. Because of the obviously dire consequences of such an unfortunate situation, one hopes for the development of fail-safe systems of protection in all international settings.

The Decision-making Team

The relationship which the decision-maker maintains with his advisors will create or destroy the opportunity for him to benefit from their multiple advocacy. The personality of the decision-maker imprints on the group either a **cautious** or an **impulsive** approach. The leader communicates his predisposition for autonomy versus dependency to his team and sets a tone of optimism or pessimism.

The advisors of the decision-maker need to view, scrutinize, and explore a full range of alternatives in order to enrich and widen the leader's perspective of a crisis. It is helpful if the advisors come from different disciplines and backgrounds and have had different molding experiences in their political development. Advisors and decision-makers need vision, flexibility, and an ability to place themselves in the adversary's position in order to understand the opposing perceptions. Decision making demands careful scrutiny of **all** the alternatives — even those which may have been initially rejected.

The team's level of efficacy will depend on team members' abilities to gather, conceive, and present alternatives. It will also depend on their willingness to avoid a **collusive pattern,** which Irving L. Janis and Leon Mann call "group think" [7]. The symptoms of this *group-think* phenomenon are:

1) the illusion of invulnerability;
2) collective efforts to rationalize situations;
3) an inherent belief in the morality of one's team;
4) a stereotypic view of rivals as being *too evil* to warrant genuine attempts at negotiation;
5) direct pressure on team members for group agreement;
6) a shared illusion of unanimity.

In a nuclear crisis — particularly an **accidental** one — such shared *group-think* would have catastrophic repercussions. The illusion of unanimity exerts pressure to conform, bolsters defensive avoidance, promotes shared rationalizations, and encourages selection of the least objectionable alternative. The decision-making team members need the moral courage to move from acquiescence to *group-think* to defiance of it when necessary. Acquiescence without the moral courage to disagree with the group can lead to dehumanization. The illusion that somebody else carries the responsibility (the *Eichman effect*) can be dangerous.

The Decision-making Process

Careful decision making widens the vision of the decision-making team by screening and sorting a broad spectrum of alternatives. The decision-making process can be viewed in terms of a five-stage paradigm:

1) the challenge is appraised;
2) the alternatives are surveyed;
3) the alternatives are weighed and evaluated;

4)   degree of commitment is deliberated;

5)   the decision is adhered to, despite negative feedback.

In a crisis, the decision-maker evaluates how serious the risks would be if he were to substitute one alternative for another. He has to determine how realistic it is to find a better alternative, and whether there is sufficient time to do so.

Wise decision making also incorporates flexibility and the willingness to reverse a decision if it proves to be immoral or shameful. In nuclear crisis, this uniquely **human** ability to be flexible and to foresee ramifications and consequences is of paramount importance.

During an actual crisis, a decision-maker and his team are burdened by the discomfort of the crisis itself. Usually, they have denied both the early signs of the on-coming upheaval and its accompanying stresses. The eruption of the crisis removes the psychologically protective cushion of denial and confronts the team with three levels of stress: (1) the urgent demand for crucial decisions in a short period of time; (2) the unsettling realization that a previously denied possibility has become a reality; and (3) an active need for creative solutions to the most pressing problems.

The process of *working through* a crisis demands from all members of the decision-making team a resilience to stress, a willingness to recognize when the stresses can no longer be handled, an awareness of levels of emotional and physical fatigue, and an ability to collaborate [8]. Crisis demands order — yet the crisis increases disorganization. Decision-makers may attempt to deal with the chaos by erroneously oversimplifying the situation and by superimposing their idealized views of what they want to see. The time limitations surrounding the crisis further foster a superficial and cursory quality of review and evaluation.

Leaders will always be affected by choice-narrowing threats. In the midst of a crisis, well-timed and unambiguous information can startle decision-makers with reality and provoke action that is equally unambiguous. A clinical example of this psychological dynamic involves a markedly obese patient who had avoided and rationalized every dietary recommendation suggested by several physicians. Only after her mother's leg was amputated because of gangrene caused by diabetes did this patient begin a strict diet and lose 45 pounds. She explained: "I could not deny my obesity any longer. My mother's stump convinced me!" [9]

Pitfalls of Decision Making

Janis and Mann have described several cognitive mechanisms by which decision-makers avoid dealing with conflict [10]. They define one such mechanism as **defensive avoidance**, which helps the decision-maker avoid the assimilation of new information by selective inattention and selective apperception [11].

Defensive avoidance blunts awareness of important clues that might surface during the crisis .

Information processing may also be impaired by a contrasting stance of **hypervigilance**, which is a state of frantic attention and awareness. A hypervigilant decision-maker and his team are unable to overview all available choices and thus have fewer options. Furthermore, any incoming information from the perceived adversary will often be interpreted as a direct threat. The hypervigilant decision-maker might even perceive a crisis where there is none and proceed to precipitate one by his overreaction.

Decision making can also be impaired or avoided by the use of **defensive procrastination** [12]. This procrastination occurs when the decision-maker (1) faces a serious threat of loss due to failure to take preventive action; (2) faces a threat of loss from taking alternative action; (3) is unable to find solutions which will reduce his losses; (4) allows the lack of pressure for a deadline to lead to inaction.

Both defensive avoidance and defensive procrastination are buttressed by selective inattention and rationalization. For example, Admiral Kimmel's failure to take preventive action at Pearl Harbor in 1941 is cited by Ned Lebow as a result of defensive avoidance [13]. Kimmel was also deprived of multiple advocacy from his advisory team when they developed a similar, collusive pattern [14]. Misperceptions in judgment also occurred when Truman ordered the crossing of the 38th parallel in Korea, during Kennedy's Bay of Pigs invasion, and with Johnson's escalation of the Viet Nam involvement.

Anger: The Ultimate Pitfall

The emotion of anger has a profound impact on the decision-making climate by promoting a tendency to view the present from the perspective of the past. The anger surrounding historical events (such as Potsdam, Munich, the 38th Parallel, Viet Nam, and probably Afghanistan) can become a prism through which perceptions and emotions of current international events and relations are viewed. For example, the Cuban Missile Crisis evoked Kennedy's reaction of anger at the Soviet leadership for apparently lying to him about the presence of the missiles in Cuba. This anger may have been responsible for Kennedy's heated reference to the fateful error in judgment made by all the participants who signed the 1938 Appeasement Pact at Munich.

Anger produces an impulse for immediate and tangible retaliation of some kind. When the USSR invaded Afghanistan in 1980, President Carter's cancellation of US participation in the Olympic Games was in part motivated by his anger at the invasion, and perhaps in part by a self-directed anger for failing to anticipate the aggression. The President was not alone in his need to demonstrate a show of anger: many people were pouring Vodka down their sinks as well!

Anger shortens reaction time, narrows the spectrum of choices, and decreases the possibility for careful assessment of the crisis. In anger, a decision-maker focuses completely on the opponent and neglects to consider his own contributions to the situation. The need to teach the adversary a lesson becomes a priority. Judgment is impaired and perceptions become skewed as secrecy abounds. Hidden stereotypes re-emerge and the ability to discern the nuances so critical in international relations is destroyed.

The feeling of anger promotes offensive rather than defensive actions and removes the possibility of understanding the opponent's self-perceptions and insecurities. Anger increases the need to show results, which in turn promotes a tendency to bluff. Bluffs create misperceptions as to the extent of the adversary's hostility. For example, Kruschev's boasts about Sputnik may have been due to his insecurity over Soviet lack of strategic parity with the US at the time. These boasts, however, only increased American determination to achieve ultimate superiority.

Bluffs increase the climate of crisis, and the accompanying response of anger makes it impossible to perceive, review, and consider the constraints under which the adversary is operating. Anger catalyzes the perception of threat and blinds decision-makers to the adversary's actual intentions. Anger is particularly dangerous in a crisis situation because it encourages an entrenchment to one's own position and promotes an insensitivity to changes in circumstances.

A decision-maker's feeling of anger can curtail vigilant assessment of the adversary's reaction. Kruschev's anger at the US's installation of the Jupiter missiles in Turkey, for example, prevented him from anticipating Kennedy's anger at the installation of Soviet missiles in Cuba.

Conclusions

The psychological factors of insensitivity, inability to retreat, defensive denial, defensive procrastination and hypervigilance affect the emotional climate of decision making, diminish the perception of choice, and transform psychosocial perceptions into misperceptions. Due to the power of these misperceptions, the same reality can be viewed very differently: "Unfortunately each person, bureaucracy, nation, views their respective perception as the only correct one." [15]

Anger, fear, and distrust internationally only serve to reinforce, intensify, and ultimately escalate the misperceptions that create the conditions for accidental nuclear war. One nation's fixation on the animosity of its adversary, together with its unwillingness to consider its own contributions to the conflict, can lead to a dangerous misreading of signs and signals.

Fostering an emotional climate of partnership in avoiding a nuclear crisis or accident would in turn facilitate a decrease in the nuclear arms race [16]. Jointly operated crisis control centers could be a fertile milieu for raising international consciousness of our mutual connectedness. We could then begin to develop partnerships between nations based on our common concerns. We could begin to explore (1) ways of meeting pressing economic and humanitarian needs (combatting world hunger and disease), (2) peaceful methods of defusing arenas of political unrest (as manifested in acts of terrorism, fanaticism, and militarism) and (3) solutions to our global environmental problems (pollution of air, water and soil). We could then expand this momentum of joint endeavors via joint ventures in space.

Global efforts in any of these areas, however, can only emerge through an emphasis on our human linkage — not through a fear of each nation's nuclear arsenals.

References

[1] Harold Nicholson, **The Congress of Vienna** (New York: Viking, 1946) p. 166

[2] Glen Fisher, **Mindsets** (International Press, 1988) p. 41

[3] Ibid., p. 41

[4] Ibid., p. 92

[5] Ned Lebow, "Who is the Enemy? Rethinking Soviet-American Relations: Why Kruschev Failed." **The Missile Crisis in Retrospect** (to be published) Chapter 5, p. 35

[6] Miroslav Nincic, "The U.S. and the Soviet Union and the Politics of Opposites" **World Politics**, 40 (1988) pp. 452-475

[7] Irving Janis & Leon Mann "A Psychological Analysis of Conflict, Choice and Commitment." **The Free Press** (1977) pp. 129-133, 179-183, 390-401, 423-430

[8] Ibid., p. 274

[9] Rita Rogers, patient communication

[10] Janis & Mann, op. cit., pp. 88-134, 434, 440-441, 442

[11] Janis & Mann, op. cit., pp. 6, 12, 87, 107, 109, 194, 205-206, 222, 224, 231-234, 238-239, 312, 323, 384

[12] Janis & Mann, op. cit., pp. 129-133, 179-180, 398-401, 423- 430

[13] Janis & Mann, op. cit., p. 398

[14] Janis & Mann, op. cit., p. 34

[15] John Spanier. "Games Nations Play", 6th ed. **Division of Congressional Quarterly**, 1987, p. 556

[16] John Stoessingers, **Nations in Darkness** (New York: Random House, 1971) p. 5

VIII. The Implications of Accidental Nuclear War: Identifying and Surmounting the Psychological Barriers to Cooperation

Morris Bradley

Although nuclear weapons have been deployed for more than forty years, there is a continued and pressing need to question whether their deployment involves risks that it is irrational to accept. The aims of this paper include five interconnected themes: 1) to argue that psychology (which in the broadest definition of the word draws on many other disciplines) has a significant role to play in understanding the past enmity between the superpowers; 2) to show that the research on risk makes it clear that our perceptions of the risks involved in deploying nuclear weapons are seriously distorted; 3) to show that the only logical conclusion, from a rational assessment of these risks, is that risk elimination is necessary rather than risk reduction; 4) to show that there is sufficient research to identify and implement the process by which the risks involved in deploying nuclear weapons could be eliminated, and that this process has an established history of success; 5) to show that formidable psychological barriers that prevent this process from being adopted have been identified.

The Contribution of Psychology

On the first theme, my assertion is that when psychological contributions are included, we now have sufficient knowledge to understand the nuclear confrontation. Since the 1950s there have been some trailblazing psychologists in several countries studying the nuclear confrontation (Frank, 1986). Also many long-established research areas in psychology can now be shown to be highly relevant (White, 1986). Psychologists have examined many aspects of the problem, such as how our thinking is imprisoned in past experience, how we are ill-equipped to deal with the rapid changes and appalling realities of the nuclear age, how weapons have been an integral part of our past culture and our need for protection so that we are trapped in a pre-nuclear mentality. There is convincing evidence about how enmity develops, how our perceptions of the enemy are distorted, and how we apply double standards in international affairs etc. etc. Without space to elaborate, my assertion remains that an impressive body of psychological research can now provide sufficient understanding of the nuclear confrontation for us to know in principle how it can be resolved.

A major difficulty of my task is that the methods of psychological research are not widely understood outside the profession, and I want the reader to be convinced that these claims can be based on credible research. I will outline just one example, chosen because it is quite memorable, can be described briefly, and deals with an elusive but crucial psychological process: psychological denial.

The Royal Society of London has published an important report on risk (Study Group on Risk Assessment, 1983), describing research that assessed the anxiety of people living at various distances from major hazards such as dams and nuclear power stations. At great distances, as would be expected, anxiety was found to increase as the distance from the danger decreased, but contrary to what most people would have predicted, the expressed anxiety peaked at 2 to 4 kilometers and then declined sharply for those living closest to the danger. From these and many other experiments it seems plausible to conclude, not only that humans can be surprisingly irrational but also that we seem able to deny realities that are too frightening to be admitted. Many psychologists believe that, in order to cope with everyday problems, people have a remarkable capacity for developing psychological denial, even suppressing from their consciousness realities that would seem to be inescapable. There is reason to believe that our biological heritage prepares us in this way to cope with frightening realities. Although some people may simply lack the imagination to understand the destructive capacity of nuclear weapons, there is evidence that fear of this causes the development of denial in early life in order to avoid feelings of despair, helplessness, and depression (Ponzo, 1986).

The Psychology of Risk

The second theme is to show how research has revealed that our perceptions of risk are seriously distorted. Although accidents occur in every area of life, it is only comparatively recently that research on risk has begun to reveal many unexpected ways in which every one of us is capable of making uncharacteristic, irrational and potentially catastrophic errors (Britten, 1983; Bradley, 1988). For example, the disaster at Chernobyl was a shock to many people because of prior assurances that the risks were negligible; but insufficient account had been taken of complex human factors, in this case leading to the deliberate decision to switch off safety devices (Hawkes, 1980).

Boredom and fatigue, especially in the low stage of the diurnal rhythm, and even the desire for excitement or bravado, can increase risks. Similarly, there is a great temptation to find ways of cutting safety procedures in order to save time or effort. More surprisingly, the need to gain social approval, or to compensate for feelings of inadequacy, can lead to irresponsibility verging on the insane (Dixon, 1987). Humans have a marked tendency to underestimate the probability that events such as indicator malfunctions can occur coincidentally, leading to false assumptions and potentially dangerous decisions. Therefore, in our assessments of risk, we are prone to fail to predict the ways in which a number of seemingly insignificant events can interact synergistically to precipitate a major disaster (Frei, 1983). In summary, human nature is very well adapted to risky behaviour but badly adapted for maintaining exemplary standards of safety. Above all, there is the need to combat complacency by remembering that human ingenuity and idiosyncracy will always generate unique and unforeseen risks.

Over the past decade important research has been done on the acceptability of risks. A *risk equation* has been defined which equates risk to the product of the probability of an accident and the severity of its consequences (Fischhoff, 1984). Most people compound these two factors, so that in everyday life we knowingly take risks that could have very serious consequences, such as death, if the probability of that occurrence is judged to be so small — for example, the probability of a road accident — that we do not believe it will happen.

However, the consequences of risks of accidents with nuclear weapons must not be dealt with in the same way as those of road accidents. Jonathan Schell (1982) was one of the first to point out that the destructive capacity of nuclear weapons puts them into an unique category: whereas, in the risk equation, the probability of an accident occurring is multiplied by a numerical representation of its severity, *we are now compelled to keep these two factors separate and distinct* The severity of the consequences of potential accidents with nuclear weapons varies from very serious to something almost unimaginable (Smoker, 1988). To become aware of the worst-case risk, we have to imagine what would happen if, unintentionally, the tens of thousands of nuclear weapons completed the destruction for which they have been designed, by launching into a full-scale attack, followed by the retaliation, and the longer-term destruction of the environment. Consequences of this order of magnitude are unprecedented and there can be no rational justification that would make them acceptable. This is true, irrespective of how small the probability of such an outcome may be — and that distinction is crucial.

It is understandable that we have the greatest difficulty in perceiving the risks involved in such extreme consequences. Linguists such as Chilton (1982) have warned us that we do not even have adequate words to describe the nuclear reality we face, since it is so unlike our previous experience. The philosopher-historian E.P.Thompson (1980) has tried to describe it as "exterminism" because it goes so far beyond previous human capacity for destructiveness. Unfortunately, people associated with nuclear weapons are not likely to ponder their decisions in terms of the rationale of the risk equation. Psychological research shows that people typically justify emotionally-charged decisions by attributing responsibility to others (Alloy, 1988).

Logical Conclusions from Risks with Nuclear Weapons

My third theme is to examine the logical conclusions that should follow from this understanding of risk. In our normal experience, when risks arise that could have serious consequences, an appropriate conclusion may be to improve the safety devices and procedures, and some of those that have been devised for nuclear weapons are quite sophisticated. However, the assurances given to the public that there are no risks at all of accidents with nuclear weapons, cannot be strictly accurate. Thousands of nuclear weapons are deployed in an immediate state of readiness, capable of being launched as a coordinated, full-scale response within a few minutes warning of a pre-emptive attack. It cannot be plausible that all the people involved in the many stages of designing, manufacturing, testing, deploying and maintaining this arsenal have superhuman infallibility, so there must be some finite probability of accidents with all of this destructive capability.

Whether those probabilities of accidents are extremely small, or whether they are much greater than is commonly believed, because of human factors and other unforeseen possibilities, the logic remains the same. The rational assessment of the consequences of such risks makes them unacceptable, no matter how small the finite probability may be. Improving safety devices and procedures is desirable but it cannot be a sufficient response to the risk. So there is only one logical conclusion; the imperative is to eliminate the probability of accidents with nuclear weapons. There is only one condition that fulfills this imperative — the probability of accidents with each weapon is eliminated when it has been dismantled or destroyed and a safe way has been found of disposing of the fissile materials (Bradley, 1988).

This logic is unlikely to be considered seriously by people in whom it raises the fear of a loss of security they perceive to be derived from the possession of nuclear weapons. Even if the logic of dismantling nuclear weapons is suggested as a possibility for some remote future date, it is still unlikely to be considered. The psychological reason for this comes from dissonance theory (Osgood, 1961), which shows that we refuse to recognize the logic of a dilemma unless we perceive that there is a viable alternative. Until people can believe that there is a convincing way in which the elimination of the nuclear weapons could be achieved, while maintaining their sense of security, the logic of the risk equation will be resisted (Flynn, 1985).

The Process By Which Nuclear Weapons Could Be Eliminated

The fourth theme is to identify the process that would result in the elimination of all nuclear weapons without destabilizing the world or threatening national security. The process is cooperation. It is my assertion that there is no problem in deciding that the process of cooperation needs to be applied, and that the practical details are manageable, but that the major difficulties lie in the psychological barriers that are preventing us from adopting this process.

The theory of cooperation has been well researched (Axelrod, 1984) and has a credible history of success in cases that seemed intractable. Often, two sides that are locked in confrontation could achieve much greater mutual benefits than are possible from the confrontation, if they could both make the change to a cooperative mode of interaction. It is possible to achieve and maintain cooperation even in conditions of deep distrust, by using verification, since the mutual benefits are usually very large compared with what can be achieved through the competitive alternative. There are many examples in the commercial world. Trust is certainly not a prerequisite for cooperation but rather grows through the experience of successful cooperation. Neither is mediation by third parties a prerequisite, though it can be decisive in facilitating a breakthrough of the psychological barriers, and mediation theory is now well-established.

Initially, cooperation develops best through a series of small steps, with full verification. The success of these often leads to a very rapid increase in the rate and scale of cooperation (Deutsch, 1986). There is no guarantee however, that cooperation can be achieved or maintained, even when the mutual benefits would obviously be much greater than those of competing. Human irrationality can very easily lead to confrontation even when the cost is high. If either side appears to the other to be seeking competitive advantage rather than cooperating, the response will probably drive both into the less successful competitive mode.

It is important to be able to distinguish between circumstances in which competition is the only option and circumstances in which cooperation offers greater rewards. Applying the theory of cooperation to the confrontation between the superpowers shows that this is certainly a case in which much greater mutual gains are possible through achieving cooperation than by confrontation. Mutual, balanced and verifiable reductions in the armed forces on both sides could release huge resources, not only of material goods but also of human potential (Bennett & Dando, 1983).

However, proving that cooperation would work in theory will not necessarily convince public opinion overnight. Happily, that is not necessary. What is needed, according to the theory, is a progression of small cooperative successes that will provide the public with the reassuring experiences that will gradually change attitudes. By this process, it becomes plausible that long before the nuclear arsenals reach some minimal level for deterrence, experiences of successful cooperation will have changed attitudes so much that total elimination of the remaining nuclear and also major offensive conventional weapons will have become a realistic and achievable goal.

Could people really feel safe without the idea of nuclear deterrence? It is probable that the enmity between the superpowers has been exacerbated by mutual fear, so success in mutual disarmament of nuclear weapons could be coupled with parallel reductions in conventional weapons to eliminate these threats also. Consider that only one generation ago, the lesson drawn from the history of hundreds of years of wars in Western Europe was always that military strength was necessary to ensure safety. This has already become an outdated way of thinking, quite inappropriate to the state of interdependence that has evolved. Competition has been restricted to the commercial field, and the network of international organizations has made nationalist wars within the European Community unthinkable for most people. These momentous changes have been much more rapid than could have been thought possible. So it is no longer implausible that changes as profound and as rapid could spread worldwide, aided by the revolution in computer and satellite communications technology, once the advantages of cooperation became apparent. Indeed, not only the risks from nuclear weapons but many other global problems necessitate the rapid development of international cooperation. Nevertheless, there are other psychological barriers to cooperation that are more complex.

The Formidable Psychological Barriers To Cooperation

The fifth theme is to identify the psychological barriers to cooperation and to show why they are so formidable. The prevailing culture in technologically advanced countries emphasizes self-interest and competition and, according to Kohn (1986), this applies especially to the United States. Attitudes that prize most highly the possibility of winning personal gain, at the loser's expense, lead to deep suspicion and often overt hostility which are incompatible with the cooperative method. Moreover, changing to cooperation cannot be done tentatively, in the sense that each decision to cooperate or compete precludes the other.

When both parties gain more by successful cooperation than they could through competition they accept equality or at least an agreeable equity. So both gain, but neither wins at the expense of the other. The aim of an agreed parity can be

115

alien to those with deeply held attitudes of rivalry. Indeed, research has shown that craving for the experience of winning and fear of being labelled a loser can make people behave with irrational competitiveness, even when it is obvious that this will incur great costs.

Our attitudes to cooperation reflect the beliefs and values that we acquire in childhood, and by which we live our lives (Rokeach, 1979). Some people see equality as an ideal that they value very highly, whereas others see it as a dangerous, or absurd notion (Ball-Rokeach, 1984). The idea of equality has also become enmeshed in political ideology. Competitive attitudes typically reflect deep childhood emotions and the most primitive of responses to other people. By contrast, the ability to inhibit competition and to cooperate when circumstances favour it, seems to develop only where favourable experiences have occurred in early life. It requires quite a complex level of understanding and self-control. The most sophisticated personality would be skilled at identifying when it is appropriate to compete and when there is more to be gained by cooperation. Such people would be the most likely to be able to induce cooperation in others, if it could be done. It is important to establish that such initiatives towards cooperation are not the same as submissive concessions which would encourage exploitation rather than cooperation. The sanction that each cooperator holds in reserve in case of defection is to revert to confrontation.

Another important psychological barrier to cooperation has already been introduced — the denial that may keep fears about nuclear weapons out of consciousness. If deterrence is believed to prevent a nuclear war from being started deliberately, denial may arise to shut out the possibility that human behaviour is not always so rational and also that there are risks in deploying nuclear weapons. In either case, denial means that there is no inducement to cooperate and no incentive to rethink the assumptions of the pre-nuclear mentality.

Yet there are those who try to cope with the reality that the future of the whole world is at risk. The difference, psychologically, in these latter is not simply that they have

116

more courage, intellectual honesty, imagination, or insight. The evidence suggests that they have gained psychological protection from the sense of helplessness and despair, and a sense of being at least partly in control of the future, as a result of taking some actions to try to help prevent the danger from occurring (Seligman, 1976; Langer, 1983). Their belief that they are right to be concerned is also supported by their knowledge that, in spite of official secrecy, evidence listing many crises, near-accidents and non-detonating accidents with nuclear weapons has been documented (Abrams, 1988).

However, recent evidence from surveys by the Canadian Institute for International Peace and Security (1988/89) found that sixty percent of Canadians, Britons, and Germans now say that it is more likely that a nuclear attack would be triggered by accident than by a deliberate, aggressive action. This suggests that, while fear of a deliberate nuclear attack by the Soviet Union is decreasing, a realization of the risk of accidents with nuclear weapons may be beginning to emerge. So denial can be overcome to some extent, by alerting ourselves to the dangers, exposing the reality, and above all trying to work towards sufficient but credible solutions.

We must also consider the implications of the probability that many people who become decision-makers in our society reach those positions primarily because of competitive attitudes that may make them unsuited to cooperation. President Eisenhower warned us that in order to change decisions affecting nuclear weapons, we must bring the talents of the public at large to bear on them.

Conclusion

As technology is changing the world so quickly, it is compelling an urgent choice between a new mode of cooperation, on this and other world problems, or the inflexible and destructive mental habits of the past. Cooperation will not emerge while the ideology of commercial rivalry is applied indiscriminately to all areas of life, treating everyone as a winner and a loser. We need to regenerate the culture that practises cooperation and understand the social value of equality. Since cooperation is learned through experience we need initiatives on every level, but especially for the children.

The nuclear confrontation is a classic case in which cooperation is the optimal, and in the long run, the only survival strategy for both superpowers. On the occasion of Mikhail Gorbachev's visit to New York to address the United Nations (*The Times*, 8 December, 1988), he likened the two superpowers to a married couple: either both can learn to share a happy marriage or both will suffer misery. This analogy is very powerful because it refers directly to a well-understood area of human experience where attitudes of winning and losing can be seen to be inappropriate.

The rewards for international cooperation are more than an escape from violence, disaster, and crippling defence budgets. Success breeds achievement just as failure breeds helplessness — the human creative potential waiting to be released is enormous and it can bring about a new Renaissance. There is no viable alternative.

References

Abrams, H. "Inescapable Risk: Human Disability and 'Accidental' Nuclear War," in: **Current Issues on Peace and Violence — Special Issue on Accidental Nuclear War** Smoker, P., and Bradley, M. eds. Nos. 1-2 (Tampere, Finland: Tampere Peace Research Institute, 1988)

Alloy, L.B. et al. "The Hopelessness Theory of Depression: Attributional Aspects," **British Journal of Clinical Psychology**, 27, 1988, pp. 5-21

Axelrod, R. **The Evolution of Cooperation** (New York: Basic Books 1984)

Ball-Rokeach, S., Rokeach, M. and Grube, J.W. **The Great American Values Test: Influencing Behavior and Belief Through Television** (New York: MacMillan, 1984)

Bennett, P. G., and Dando, M. R. "The Arms Race: Is It Just a Mistake?" **New Scientist**, Feb.17, 1983, pp. 432-435

Bradley, M. "The Application of Psychology to Problems of Nuclear Confrontation and the Risk of Accidental Nuclear

War" in: **Current Issues on Peace and Violence- Special Issue on Accidental Nuclear War** Smoker, P., and Bradley, M. eds. Nos. 1-2 (Tampere, Finland: Tampere Peace Research Institute, 1988)

Bradley, M. and Smoker, P. "Logical Implications of the Risk of Accidental Nuclear War and Concomitant Psychological Factors" in: **Current Issues on Peace and Violence— Special Issue on Accidental Nuclear War** Smoker, P., and Bradley, M. eds. Nos. 1-2 (Tampere, Finland: Tampere Peace Research Institute, 1988)

Britten, S. **The Invisible Event** (London: Menard, 1983)

Chilton, P. "Nukespeak: Nuclear Language, Culture and Propaganda" in: **Nukespeak, The Media and the Bomb** (London: Comedia Minority Press, 1982)

Deutsch, M. "Strategies of Inducing Cooperation" in: **Psychology and the Prevention of Nuclear War** White, R.K. ed. (New York: University Press, 1986)

Dixon, N.E. **Our Own Worst Enemy** (London: Trinity Press, 1987)

Fenton, I. ed. **The Psychology of Nuclear Conflict** (London: Coventure, 1986)

Fischhoff, B., Lichtenstein, S., Slovic, P., Derby, S.L. and Keeney, R.L. **Acceptable Risk** (London: Cambridge University Press, 1984)

Flynn, G., and Rattinger, H. eds. **The Public and Atlantic Defense** (London: Croom Helm, 1985)

Frank, J.D. "Pre-Nuclear Age Leaders and the Nuclear Arms Race" in: **The Psychology of Nuclear Conflict** Fenton, I. ed. (London: Coventure, 1986)

Frei, D. **Risks of Unintentional Nuclear War** (New Jersey: Allenheld, Osmun, 1983)

Hawkes, N. et al. **The Worst Accident in the World: Chernobyl, The End of the Nuclear Dream** (London: Pan Books, 1986)

Kohn, A. **No Contest: The Case Against Competition** (Houghton Mifflin, 1986)

Langer, E.J. **The Psychology of Control** (Sage, 1983)

Osgood, C.E. "An Analysis of the Cold War Mentality," **Journal of Social Issues** 17(3), 1961 pp. 17-19.

119

Ponzo, E. et al. "Italian Adolescents Concerns about the Threat of Nuclear War," **Proceedings of the International European Psychologists for Peace** Conference, Helsinki, 1986

Rokeach, M. **Understanding Human Values** (New York: Free Press, 1979)

Royal Society Report on Risk Assessment, Royal Society, London, 1983

Schell, J. **The Fate of the Earth** (Picador, 1982)

Seligman, M.E.P. & Maier, S.F. "Learned Helplessness, Theory and Evidence: A Review," **Journal of Experimental Psychology**, 1976, p. 105

Smoker, P. "Accidental Nuclear Winter: Implications for Deterrence" in: **Current Issues on Peace and Violence — Special Issue on Accidental Nuclear War** Smoker, P., and Bradley, M. eds. Nos. 1-2. (Tampere, Finland: Tampere Peace Research Institute, 1988)

Thompson, E.P. & Smith, D. **Protest and Survive** (London: Penguin Books, 1980)

White, R. K. **Psychology and the Prevention of Nuclear War** (New York: University Press, 1986)

IX. International Tension and the Chance of Accidental Nuclear War

Paul Smoker and Ib Petersen

Introduction: Less than Eight Minutes

On Sunday July the 3rd 1988 the Aegis cruiser USS Vincennes and the frigate USS Elmer Montgomery were on patrol in the western curve of the Gulf near the straight of Hormuz. Tension had been high in the area for some time and spectacular military action was expected on the following day (July 4). Early in the morning the Vincennes dispatched a helicopter to investigate between 13 and 15 Iranian patrol boats. At 6.10 GMT the patrol boats opened fire on the helicopter and both warships sailed to the scene. At 6.42 GMT they fired their 12.7 cm guns at the Iranian boats. The Pentagon claimed two Iranian gunboats were sunk and a third damaged.

At 6.47 GMT the Aegis surface to air missile system on the Vincennes detected an aircraft over Iran heading out over the water. The $525 million Aegis system is a part of the most advanced naval combat system in the world, it is capable of tracking the speed, course and radar signature of more than 200 targets at a range of up to 400 kilometers. It can also attack up to 20 targets simultaneously and comprises a complex command and control system incorporating high speed computers, four radar screens, simulated voices giving audio updates and real time tracking of events.

At 6.49 GMT the Vincennes sent the first of at least six radio warnings to the aircraft on various frequencies. It was heading towards the Vincennes at 800 kilometers per hour. At 6.51 GMT the Vincennes declared the plane hostile, believing it to be a US built Iranian F-14 twin engined supersonic fighter. At 6.52 an Iran Air Airbus A300 exploded 2,250 metres over the Straights of Hormuz seven minutes after take off. At least one of the two Standard missiles fired by the Vincennes hit the jet at a distance of 10 kilometers from the ship. All 290 people on the airbus died.

The Iranians claimed that the plane had been flying "precisely in the international corridor" and that, "Considering the regular and repeated flight of passenger planes through this international corridor, the American fleet should have been quite familiar with this route." [1]

This paper argues that such accidents are inevitable when complex human-computer command and control systems operate under extreme time pressure, and that the probability of error is directly proportional to the level of perceived tension. It builds upon extensive earlier work that is reviewed elsewhere (Smoker and Bradley, 1988) in describing the results of an ongoing project that is elaborated in a monograph-length manuscript (Petersen and Smoker, 1989). The 1989 manuscript presents a quantitative analysis of the relationship between international tension and Threat Evaluation Conferences (TECs) in the NORAD C^3I system for nuclear weapons.

Indexing International Tension and C^3I Errors

Tension between the super-powers is indexed using the World Event Interaction Study (**WEIS**) data for the years 1977-78. WEIS procedures were adopted because they represent an established and widely accepted method for measuring international tension. WEIS uses the New York Times, the London Times and the Los Angeles Times as sources and codes international events reported in these sources. Two new WEIS type event data sets, **IBDATA1** and **IBDATA2**, were also created. **IBDATA1** uses WEIS coding procedures for the years 1978-84 since the WEIS series stops in 1978. IBDATA1 used just the New York Times, since relative rather than absolute numbers are of interest here [2]. In order to have a parallel indicator of official US perceptions of the USSR the US "Department of State Bulletin" (DSB) was similarly event coded for the years 1977-84. This created the second new dataset IBDATA2 in which the US is the actor and the USSR is the target.

While event data provide a relatively fine-grain basis for indexing levels of international tension, a number of macro-tension indicators are also available including the **defence ratio** used here for the years 1977-84. The defence ratio compares levels of expenditure on armaments relative to GNP. The defence ratio is a crude indicator of international tension.

Data on the frequency of Threat Assessment Conferences (TACs), Threat Evaluation Conferences (TECs) and Routine Missile Display Conferences (RMDCs) at NORAD are also available for 1977-84. A thorough investigation revealed that TACs, the most serious type of conference, had too low a frequency for statistical purposes, six such conferences being convened during the whole period. RMDCs were sufficiently frequent but were unsuitable and unreliable due to definitional problems and operational procedures and changes.

TECs, which are convened if the C^3I system indicates the possibility of a threat to the USA, are used in this paper as an indicator of erroneous messages in the C^3I system (the possibility of a genuine attack on the USA when no such attack existed). The frequencies of TECs during the period under consideration are adequate, varying between 40 and 255 per year. Desmond Ball [3] takes the view that :

"There were technical explanations of all six TACs which have nothing to do with the state of verbal tension, but rather with computer shake-downs and Soviet missile tests.

"I believe that similar explanations apply to the pattern of Threat Evaluation Conferences (TECs), and to the peaking of TECs in 1981-83. First there were developments in US sensor systems which yielded unusual information. For example, the first two Pave Paws SLBM warning radars became operational in 1980-81 and began producing data on SLBM test trajectories which had hitherto not been available. Similarly, the DSP satellite launched in July 1981 carried an improved sensor which generated new types of data concerning SLBM launches.

"The second explanation concerns Soviet ICBM and SLBM test launches. Almost all TECs are associated with a Soviet test launch. This is particularly the case for tests from operational silos, (ie not Pletsk or Tyuratam) and submarines. .... NORAD duty officers are not so much concerned with missiles fired from the test ranges as with missiles fired from operational silos and submarines."

The present paper challenges Ball's view that TECs "have nothing to do with the state of verbal tension" and argues that perceived international tension is related to the frequency of TECs during this period. The paper concludes by considering the relationship between TACs, TECs and the probability of an accidental or unintended nuclear war.

Table 1: List of Variables

DSB: US accusations found in The Department of State Bulletin.

TEC: yearly aggregates of Threat Evaluation Conferences.

DR : The defense ratio.

NCO: US - USSR consultations.

NUS: US accusations towards USSR.

NSU: USSR accusations towards US

NCU: US accusations towards USSR minus US - USSR consultations.

NCS: USSR accusations towards US minus US - USSR consultations.

NCA: US+USSR accusations.

NCC: NCA - NCO

Graphic Analysis - Observations on Figures.

The following figures are designed to illustrate variation and co-variation between variables. The data have been standardized in such a way that the minimum value for each variable is zero and the maximum is 100.

124

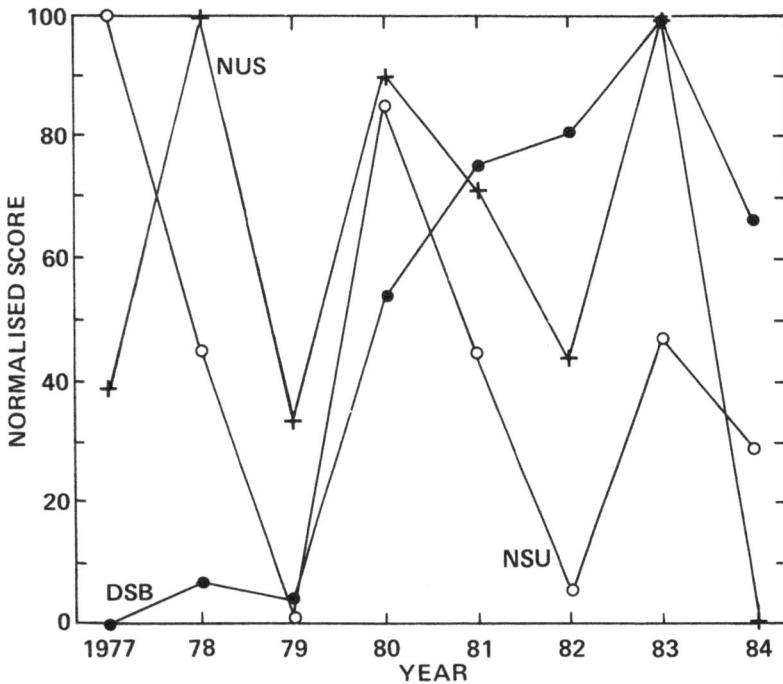

Figure 1: Governmental and News World Indicators of Tension

During the period 1977-84, US and USSR accusations as indexed by NUS and NSU, WEIS type event data indicators generated from an analysis of the New York Times, do not rise and fall with DSB, an analogous indicator of US accusations generated from the Department of State Bulletin. NUS and NSU are based on many fewer observations and thus are more unstable than DSB. DSB is based on a very large number of observations and is probably a stable indicator of US governmental verbal aggression and perceptions of international tension. The New York Times it can be argued provides a more *detached* measure of international tension than the Department of State Bulletin in the sense that it is based on journalist's interpretations of events rather than the interpretation of the actual decision-makers or their associates.

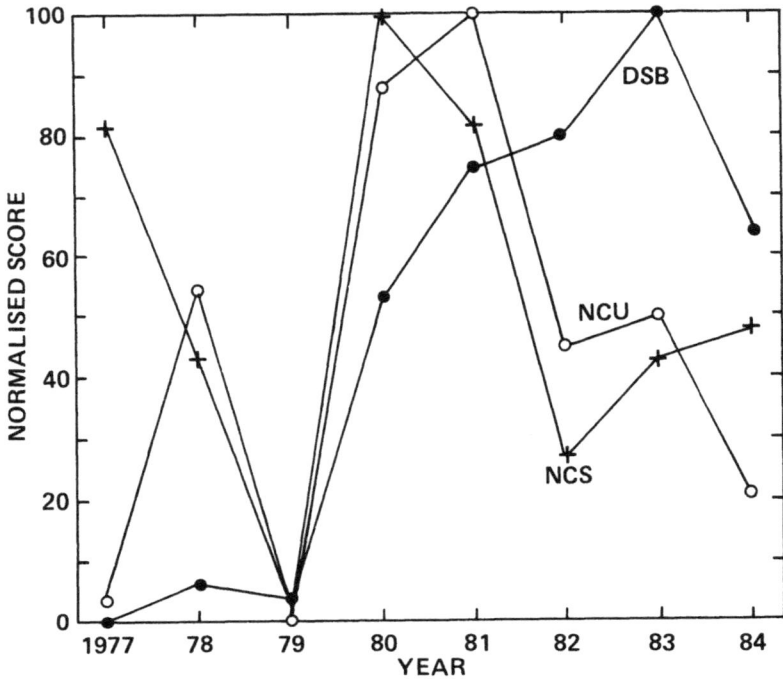

Figure 2: Indicators of US and USSR Aggressiveness

Figure 2 shows the more *detached* News World indicators of US aggressiveness towards the Soviet Union (NCU); and USSR aggressiveness towards the United States (NCS); together with the Department of State Bulletin indicator of US aggressiveness DSB. The two *detached* indicators rise and fall together during the period 1978-83, but move in opposite directions during the first and last years of the period. From this perspective, the two highest tension years were 1980 and 1981, reflecting the crisis over Afghanistan. The high NCS level for 1977 should also be noted. Again there is no connection between these two News World indicators of international tension and the level of US aggressiveness observed in the Department of State Bulletin, except for the Carter period 1977-80 where NCU and DSB move together.

126

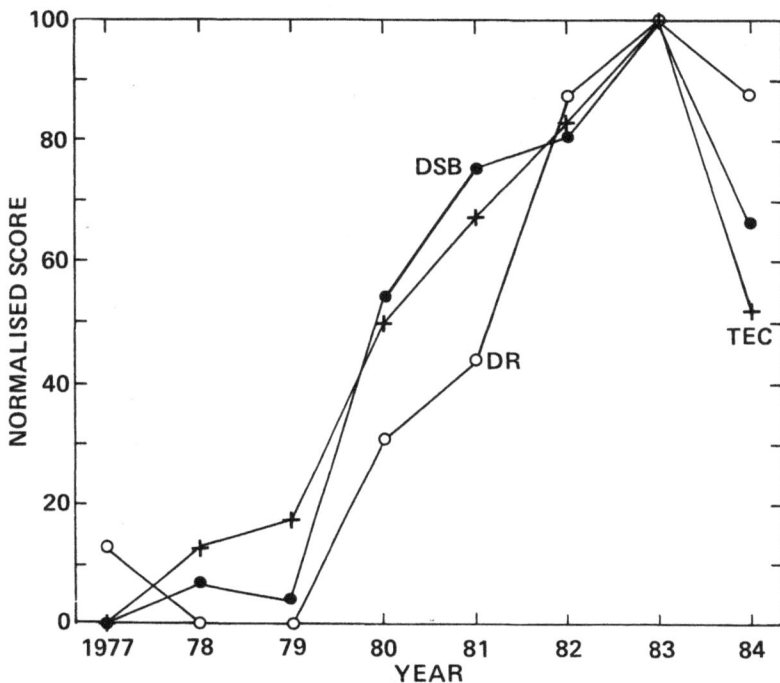

Figure 3: DR, DSB and Threat Evaluation Conferences, TEC

This remarkable diagram shows the covariation of the defense ratio (DR), US governmental verbal aggression (DSB) and frequencies of Threat Evaluation Conferences (TEC). They rise and fall despite the fact that the indicators were drawn from different sources by three different people without any prior connection and brought together in this study. This diagram suggests there may be some underlying structure that connects US governmental perceptions of tension as expressed in the Department of State Bulletin, the calling of Threat Evaluation Conferences and US defense expenditure as compared with total governmental expenditure. It is possible that the apparent linkage between these three variables is spurious and for this reason, although there are insurmountable statistical problems inherent in the small number of time points, it is possible to undertake a correlational analysis that complements the visual impressions.

Correlational Analysis

Table 2: Correlations of Main Variables

Variable	Time	TEC	DR	DSB	NUS	NSU	CON
Time		83	91	87	-21	-43	-45
TEC	83		88	97	14	-28	-48
DR	91	88		90	-14	-26	-33
DSB	87	97	90		14	-21	-57
NUS	-21	14	-14	14		32	-3
NSU	-43	-28	-26	-21	32		1
CON	-45	-48	-33	-57	-3	1	

(All correlations are multiplied by 100).

Were true time series data available in the unclassified literature on the occurrence of TECs then it would be possible to undertake a relatively reliable time series analysis of the relationship between all the indicators, with the exception of the defence ratio, using the disagregated events data [4].

Here we are limited to the use of a correlational analysis. Consequently the inferences drawn in the following section must be treated with considerable caution since the potential for error in such a small sample is substantial.

The three central variables in this study all intercorrelate at 0.83 or above. These three variables are the frequency of Threat Evaluation Conferences (TEC), the Defence Ratio (DR), and the number of verbal accusations by high ranking officials reported in the Department of State Bulletin (DSB). The probability of obtaining a correlation of 0.83 or above in an uncorrelated population of statistics is less than 0.01. None of the other variables manifest such high correlations. Only the three central variables have correlations of 0.83 or above with time.

These results are consistent with the assumption that during the period 1977 to 1984 there is a relationship between the level of perceived international tension, as inferred from the verbal accusations of leading US decision-makers, and the frequency of mistakes in the North American Air Defence (NORAD) system, as indexed by TECs. There is no such relationship if the more detached WEIS indicators NUS and NSU are used.

In order to explore the relationship between these variables further, partial correlations were used to remove the correlation with time. When this was done the linkage between TEC and DSB remains at a level that would be significant at the 0.01 level in an uncorrelated population of statistics, the partial correlation being 0.90. DR gives partial correlations of 0.53 with DSB and 0.54 with TEC, figures that are beneath the 0.05 level of 0.71 for an uncorrelated population of statistics.

Thus while all three central variables may be correlated in time and are possibly related indicators of the psycho-political dynamics of the period, TEC and DSB are perhaps also linked independent of time. This is consistent with the hypothesis that US Governmental perceptions of international relations, as indexed by DSB, are linked to errors in the command and control systems, as indexed by TEC, independent of genuine computer generated incidents.

The DSB indicator is based on statements by the President, Vice President, Secretaries of State, and other important lower level decision-makers. If these categories are treated as separate variables then *others* correlates 0.98 with the Total DSB, while the President correlates 0.81. Similarly *others* correlates 0.98 with Threat Evaluation Conferences (TEC) while the President correlates 0.78. Like the threats and accusations generated by *others*, Threat Evaluation Conferences were generated by important lower level decision-makers in the NORAD command and control centre who at the time perceived a possible attack on the United States.

It is possible that the psychological linkage between TEC and DSB is in part related to the attributes and decision-making environments of these important lower level decision-makers. If the 0.98 correlation of *others* with TEC is partialed to remove the effects of time then the resulting correlation of 0.93 is even higher than the already high 0.90 generated by time partialed DSB. For the President component of DSB the partial is 0.30. Decision makers *other* than those at the very highest level provide a relevant context for further exploration of this most important phenomenon. We will return to this possibility when discussing TECs, TACs and the probability of nuclear war.

Four Phases: TECs, TACs and the Probability of Nuclear War

If the *detached* and DSB indicators in figures 1 to 3 are compared then four distinct phases can be identified.

Phase 1: 1977-1979 Conciliatory/Provocative. The Carter administration, it can be argued, under-responded to the level of international tension perceived by *detached* commentators. During this period four of the six most serious C^3I conferences, Threat Assessment Conferences (TACs), occurred at the rate of two each year during 1978 and 1979 despite the low level of Threat Evaluation Conferences (TECs). This reaction in the nuclear command and control system should be seen in conjunction with USSR aggressiveness in Africa and Afghanistan. The under-response of the Carter administration during 1977-79 in terms of verbal aggressiveness towards the Soviet Union can perhaps be seen as a deliberate policy to ensure the signing of the SALT 2 agreement in July 1979, which was responded to by the USSR with a very low level of aggression in 1979 in contradistinction to its initial high level of aggressiveness in 1977. This phase is in some ways a mirror image of the years 1982-83 for the Soviet Union and will be referred to again in our discussion of TECs, TACs and the probability of nuclear war.

Phase 2: 1979-81 Realistic   Two TACs occurred in each of the years 1979 and 1980; but 149 TECs were recorded in 1980 — a near-doubling of the 78 TECs recorded in 1979. Following the Soviet intervention in Afghanistan US actions were realistic in the sense that the rate of change in DSB accusations towards the USSR was commensurate with the rate of change in what can be seen as *detached* indicators.

Phase 3 1981-83 Provocative/Conciliatory   No TACs have been reported for the period 1981-84, a period

130

during which the frequency of TECs rises to a maximum and then falls. The US governmental verbal aggressiveness seems to depart radically from the level of international tension perceived by *detached* observers. Accusations in the DSB rise to a maximum while *detached* indicators (NCU and NCC) move downward. This political posture is linked with an increase in the defense ratio. The years 1982-83 mark a high point in hostility to the Soviet Union and in US governmental aggressiveness. They culminate with the adoption of SDI, the empire of evil speech, accusations connected with the downing of a Korean airliner, and an alleged Soviet near panic almost triggering an accidental nuclear war. In phase 3, it can be argued, a deliberate policy of confrontation created the impression of a crisis-like situation. A number of examples illustrate this situation. In 1984 an International Peace and Friendship Caravan visited Europe. A Polish Captain, chairman of the Polish Peace Committee in Gdansk wrote in the diary of one of the Canadian participants that there were 146 malfunctions in the Soviet Defense System (presumably in 1983) six of which were extremely serious. In the terms of this paper these figures may to some extent correspond to 140 Soviet TECs and 6 Soviet TACs. He also wrote that it takes on average 20 minutes to track down errors.

This example provides us with one possible hypothesis to link TECs, TACs and the probability of a nuclear war, although lacking as we do good indicators for Soviet equivalents of DSB, TECs and TACs any hypothesis concerning the relationship between TACs, TECs and the probability of nuclear war is at the present time purely speculative. The evidence presented in this paper certainly suggests that, contrary to the opinion of Desmond Ball, the frequency of TECs may be related to the state of verbal tension. The following hypothesis is presented to illustrate one possible pattern that can be explored further by future research. A broad range of alternatives is explored in a forthcoming paper.

Phases 1 and 3, it can be argued, may be in a psychological sense mirror images of each other. During such periods one of the actors pursues a confrontational policy, with an

131

associated increase in TECs since important but lower level decision-makers are involved in TECs and the tension associated with such a phase is a factor that can, as in the case of the Vincennes incident, cause such decision-makers to interpret patterns of events, including technical malfunctions, unusual information, or operational missile tests as potentially hostile. The correlational evidence, it should be remembered, suggested such a possibility.

The other actor will be more likely to generate the more serious TAC type errors because of the aggressiveness and hostility of the potential adversary and the apparently real threat this poses. In phase three, from 1981 to 1983, we would therefore anticipate a higher probability of TAC type errors in the Soviet system, as was the case in the NORAD system during phase 1.

Similarly during a period such as phase 2, where all indicators move up together, we would expect an increase in TECs in the command and control systems of both actors, as well as a higher probability of TAC type errors in both command and control systems, if the Soviet equivalent of DSB also moved up. Two TACs occurred in the NORAD system during this phase as did a close to doubling of the frequency of TECs in the NORAD system. In phase four as defined below we would expect a reduction in TECs and a lower probability of TAC type errors in both C^3I systems since all indicators of verbal aggression moved downwards.

This hypothesis would argue that, all other things being equal, the probability of a nuclear war will be higher in a phase 2 type situation since TAC type errors are more likely to occur on both sides, and TEC type errors associated with perceived increasing hostility of the other actor are likely to increase. This argument conforms to the view that the probability of nuclear war increases substantially during a crisis where the interaction between the C^3I systems can under worst case analysis generate a self-exciting situation.

In addition it suggests an increase in the probability of nuclear war during situations such as phases 1 or 3 where the aggressiveness of the first actor is associated with an increase in first actor TECs and the probability of second actor TACs

In fact there is further evidence to support this hypothesis with regard to phase 3.

A Korean airliner was shot down near a Soviet Pacific coast base in August 1983 after reportedly being mistaken for an American RC 135 reconnaissance plane. Tension had been generated in the area for months as the US Navy had started what were for the Soviets highly provocative maneuvers called Fleetex in April. Fleetex was a battle exercise involving a north Pacific *armada* of three aircraft carriers and forty-one escorts plus land based naval and Air Force planes from Guam, Adak, Japan and the US West Coast. Held back-to-back with Team Spirit , a 1983 practice run for war against north Korea involving 188,000 US and South Korean Navy, Air Force and Army forces, Fleetex reasserted US presence in the northwest Pacific up to a hundred kilometers off the Soviet coast less than twenty minutes flight time for carrier strike aircraft. This exercise in the Soviet Union's *backyard* was aimed, as Commander of the Pacific Fleet Admiral Foley put it, at "taunting the Soviet Pacific Fleet".

Shortly after KAL 007 was shot down the US and Japan conducted their largest joint maneuvers since World War II in the Sea of Japan. This exercise involved 150 Japanese ships and 30,000 Japanese military personnel along with two US aircraft carriers and escorts. Planned long before the tragedy, the exercise nonetheless exacerbated Soviet tension. In what the US press described as "highly provocative" maneuvers, the forces practiced blockading the Tsugaru and Tsushima Straits against Soviet ships leaving their headquarters at Vladivostok.

Mrs Suzanne Massie, an expert on Russian History and author of several books on old Russia, was in Moscow after the shooting down of the Korean airliner. She was approached by a Soviet official who told her: "You don't know how close war is". This official asked her to convey this message to US President Reagan which eventually she did.

Former Soviet spy Oleg Gordievski, who worked for British intelligence for ten years, alleges that on November 8-9 1983 "the Kremlin came close to pressing the panic button" [5] as a result of a secret NATO nuclear weapon

133

exercise called Able Archer. "Moscow's KGB intelligence headquarters issued a nuclear attack alert to its overseas agents in November 1983. The alert instructed agents to watch for unusual activity that could confirm suspicions that a strike was being prepared against the Soviet Union. The danger was increased by Paranoia in the Kremlin."

Phase 4 1984 Realistic All indicators (except NUS and NSU) point towards a relaxation of tension and once more a political attitude commensurate with the situation.

Conclusion

This paper argues that levels of international tension and the frequency of Threat Evaluation Conferences are linked during the period 1977-1984. It further suggests that the probability of nuclear war is likely to increase not only during a crisis-type situation, such as the period 1980-81, but also during periods of asymmetry such as 1978-80 and 1981-83. Further research is needed to explore this possibility.

Notes

[1] The Japanese Times, 2nd Edition, Tuesday, July 5, 1988.
[2] It has been shown that about 10% of WEIS data are from journals other than NYT.
[3] Personal communication, July 14, 1989.
[4] It is our hope that through the good offices of Lt. General Lloyd R. Leavitt Jr. (ret) it will be possible for NORAD to use our events data to undertake a study.
[5] Details given in **Nuclear Alert: International Accidental Nuclear War Prevention Newsletter**, Vol. 5, No. 1, Winter 1988-89.

Bibliography

Lebow, Richard N, **Between Peace and War: The Nature of International Crisis** (Baltimore: Johns Hopkins University Press, 1981)
Lebow, Richard N , **Nuclear Crisis Management: A Dangerous Illusion** (Ithaca N.Y.: Cornell University, 1987)

Petersen, Ib and Paul Smoker, **The Effect of International Tension on the Probability of Accidental Nuclear War** (Canterbury, New Zealand: Department of Sociology, University of Canterbury, 1989)

Smoker, Paul , "Trade, Defence and the Richardson Theory of Arms Races: A Seven Nation Study" **Journal of Peace Research,** pp. 161-176, No. 2, 1965

Smoker, Paul and Morris Bradley (eds), "Accidental Nuclear War", complete volume of **Current Research on Peace and Violence,** Vol. 1, No, 2 (1988) Tampere Peace Research Institute, Finland, pp. 1-79

X. Disabled Leaders, Cognition and Crisis Decision Making

Herbert L. Abrams

Much of the analytic framework that supports national policy — for example, deterrence theory — is based on the assumption of human rationality and predictable decision making. The theory is that rational man will choose the best possible course after weighing the probabilities and the potential gains and losses of alternative courses of action.

If this is how decisions should be made, it is not necessarily how they *are* made. Decision making in foreign policy is not a science. Often, the fog of hope and wishful thinking obscures the facts. Nations miscalculate and go to war believing that national goals will surely be attained. In the recent past, this was true of Iraq's attack on Iran; the US in Viet Nam; the USSR in Afghanistan; and Viet Nam's invasion of Cambodia. All of these major national decisions proved to be catastrophes. The great fiascoes in US foreign policy have resulted from human errors in assessing situations that involved other countries. The Bay of Pigs, Pearl Harbor, and the escalation of the Viet Nam War each can be used to exemplify failure in our top decision-making processes.

Decision making in crisis has been subjected to careful assessment. Such studies have demonstrated major perceptual problems [1-3], narrowing of the cognitive process [4], increasing errors under the pressure of time [5], and a group dynamic that ultimately substitutes consensual validation for critical assessment [6]. The degradation of the analytic process reflects the confluence of many factors, including the quality and quantity of available information, the powerful effects of stress, the strength of individual needs, and the personality traits of the leadership [7].

Most studies of crisis behavior have accepted the premise that it represents the response of *normal* or *stable* individuals to stress. The assumption of rational decision making loses credibility, then, if the behavior of an individual, who is generally thought to be stable, changes significantly in crisis, as we know it does; and perhaps more significantly, if the leadership responsible for decisions in crisis is impaired by physical, psychological, or drug-induced disability.

It is timely, therefore, to define the demography of disease in national leaders, the cognitive effects of the disorders to which they are subject, and their potential impact on the capacity to cope with complexity. We focus on organic illness because there is a large and reasonably accurate record available for analysis.

The Demography of Organic Illness: US Presidents of the Century

Thirteen of the seventeen US presidents in the 20th century have had significant and numerous illnesses while in office. Franklin D. Roosevelt (FDR) and Harding died; and Wilson, FDR, Eisenhower, Johnson, and Reagan were incapacitated by illness and/or surgery. There were seven assassination attempts on the seventeen presidents, two successful (McKinley and Kennedy). Three presidents (Wilson, Coolidge, and Johnson) died within four years after leaving office [8].

McKinley, Taft, Wilson, Harding, Coolidge, FDR, Truman, Eisenhower, and Johnson suffered from heart disease, ranging from thin heart walls to progressive arteriosclerosis. Taft, Wilson, Harding, FDR, and Eisenhower had high blood pressure.

T. Roosevelt, FDR, Truman, Eisenhower, Johnson, and Reagan underwent surgery at least once. Wilson, Harding, FDR, and Eisenhower experienced strokes. FDR, Johnson, and Reagan had forms of cancer. Truman, Eisenhower, and Johnson had gall bladder disease. Wilson and Johnson had kidney disease.

Wilson, Harding, Coolidge, FDR, Truman, Eisenhower, and Kennedy suffered from gastrointestinal disorders, ranging from ulcers and enzyme deficiency to chronic inflammatory bowel disease.

T. Roosevelt, Coolidge, Wilson, FDR, and Johnson

suffered from various kinds of chronic respiratory illness.

Other major health problems included diabetes (Harding), Addison's Disease (Kennedy), prostatic disease (Wilson and Reagan), phlebitis (Nixon), periodic alcohol abuse (Harding, Nixon, and Johnson), and obesity (McKinley, Taft, Harding, and Johnson).

Soviet Leaders

Five Soviet leaders died while in office: Lenin, Stalin, Brezhnev, Andropov, and Chernenko. The longest interregnum (1953-1957) followed Stalin's death. The period between 1979 and 1985 was particularly marked by disabled and incapacitated leadership.

While in office, Lenin and Andropov underwent surgery. Four of the seven Soviet leaders suffered from serious heart conditions: Lenin, Stalin, Brezhnev, and Andropov [8]. Three had strokes: Lenin (four); Stalin (three); Brezhnev (one or two). Three (Lenin, Stalin and Brezhnev) and possibly four (Khrushchev) had hypertension.

Lenin was shot, had four strokes, massive cerebral arteriosclerosis, and coronary arteriosclerosis.

Stalin had coronary and cerebral arteriosclerosis and experienced three strokes.

Khrushchev suffered from heart disease and had a number of heart attacks.

Brezhnev had widespread arteriosclerosis, severe coronary disease, cardiac arhythmias, strokes, aneurysm of the abdominal aorta, gout, leukemia, and emphysema.

Andropov experienced a heart attack, chronic kidney failure, diabetes, and hypertension.

Chernenko had chronic hepatitis and cirrhosis, heart disease, pneumonia, emphysema, and bronchitis.

Space does not permit a catalogue of the diseases affecting other national leaders — such as Churchill, Eden, and Pompidou — while in office.

Cognitive Effects of Organic Disease

This brief summary permits a catalogue of the diseases and organic insults that have most commonly affected U.S. and Soviet leaders:

- heart disease   - strokes
- trauma   - surgery
- cancer   - gastrointestinal disease
- drugs   - blood loss

Heart disease. A heart attack is a life-threatening, acute illness that frequently occurs without much warning. Following a heart attack, anxiety, depression, difficulty in concentration, and problems with sleep occur in a large percentage of patients [9, 10]. Four months after the attack, over half the patients have psychological disturbances [11], and depression persists [12, 13]. One-third of patients studied after an interval of 6-26 months were subject to such problems as fatigue, impaired memory, inability to concentrate, emotional instability, and irritability [14]. The presence of heart disease by itself has been found to be a predictor of significant intellectual disability [15]. Even the diagnosis of heart disease may cause detectable depression over a three-year period [16].

Strokes. Depression, anxiety, and emotional lability characterize many patients after stroke [17]. Between 41% and 62% of patients are cognitively and emotionally impaired; 97% suffer from headaches, with memory loss in 28% [18]. Depression may remain severe 6 months to 2 years after the stroke [19-21]. Insomnia and feelings of hopelessness are manifest [22].

Trauma. Anxiety, difficulty in concentrating, and memory impairment are observed in patients following trauma. There are feelings of intense helplessness and loss of control [23]. Physicians and nurses are accustomed to seeing disturbances in the organization of thought [24]. Depression, perplexity, flightiness, and excessive dependence are commonly noted [23-25].

Surgery. One of the sequelae of major surgery is

confusion severe enough to impede the patient's ability to think clearly. It may be associated with impaired memory and disorientation in time, space, and with people. Post-surgical patients may lose the ability to grasp concepts and to use deductive and inductive logic. The elderly are especially susceptible to confusion. Depression, anger and anxiety occur in many. Among those over 65, a 50% incidence of disabling post-operative depression has been reported [26-28].

Cancer. Depression is the most common emotional complication of cancer [29-31]. It is accompanied by anxiety, regressive behavior, and anger [31-32]. The chemotherapeutic drugs that patients receive may also produce profound cognitive impairment [30, 33].

Hypertension. Depression, anxiety, irritability, emotional instability, memory loss, difficulty in concentration, insomnia, fatigue, and shortened attention span are frequently found in patients with hypertension, particularly when it is accompanied by cerebral arteriosclerosis [17, 34, 35]. Patients are prone to judgmental deficits, hopelessness, and sometimes depression. Slowness in comprehension, labored thinking, faulty orientation, memory impairment, and slowed mental processing have been demonstrated by standard psychometric tests [36, 37].

Hypertensive patients on medication perform significantly more slowly than do individuals with normal blood pressure [35].

Blood loss. Both surgery and trauma may be accompanied by major blood loss and may produce a state of shock. If blood loss is severe, oxygen deprivation may occur. Headache, fatigue, and inability to concentrate characterize decreased oxygen availability [38]. The performance of complex tasks is impaired [39].

Drugs. The drugs that presidents and leaders receive for their illnesses are many and varied. If they undergo surgery, the anesthetics themselves may have sustained hangover effects, may be amnestic, and may take many days to be eliminated from their bodies. The anesthetics may induce inhibitions, or encourage over-confidence. Even in young, healthy subjects, physiologic effects are still detectable many hours after anesthesia [40, 41].

The opiates, frequently administered during and after surgery, are accompanied by drowsiness, mental clouding, and a sense of detachment [41]. Elderly patients may be particularly sensitive [42].

The Potential Impact of Cognitive Alterations on Decision Making

Cognition is the sophisticated interaction of mental processes that produces human thought. Among the host of functions embodied by cognition are concentration, attention, inventiveness, intuition, memory, foresight, reflection, deliberation, inference, speculation, discrimination, recognition, comprehension, evaluation, deductive and inductive reasoning, and abstract and logical thought. All are applicable to meaningful decision making, and many are essential when the time for decision making is shortened. Under the pressure of time, there is a heightened need to make measured assessments, to weigh evidence, to be rational, to remember, and to organize and integrate information from disparate sources promptly and effectively. "Problem solving involves the manipulation in consciousness of alternatives, choices, probable and possible outcomes and consequences, and alternative goals" [43].

But the *sick state* is characterized by regression and withdrawal [44]. Attention is drawn inward and mental energies are devoted to dealing with the concerns evoked by the disease.

Depression, so common an effect of illness, is associated with self-doubt and avoidance of decisions or acceptance of responsibility [45, 46]. When depressed individuals can be induced to make decisions, their capabilities are reduced. They have impaired attention, concentration, and memory. Their powers of analysis fail, and they may over-emphasize negative information [47].

The anxiety that so commonly characterizes all of these illnesses degrades learning and memory. Ability to reason is impaired [48].

141

A common consequence of illness and of surgery is confusion, to which elderly individuals are particularly prone. In a confused state, memory and logical thought are disrupted. There is an "inability to maintain either a coherent stream of thought or an ordered sequence of goal directed behavior" [26].

A manifest overlap exists between the cognitive effects of organic disease and those of stress [2]. This is hardly surprising because stress is both a cause of disease and a product of it. When the stress that surrounds a crisis is heightened by the effects of illness, the capacity to respond may be profoundly impaired. Sound decision making requires a consistent perception of the utility of an outcome. But perceptions of utility may be drastically altered by pain or discomfort, which act as "interrupters", demanding the individual's attention [6]. Of equal importance, the information handling capacities of the sick leader are diminished.

In both the national and the leader's interest, he should be separated from the burden of decision making in crisis.

Prescriptive Implications

The most serious obstacle to determining presidential disability has been the misguided attempt by advisors to hide news of the health and stability of the leader from the public. The extraordinary measures taken by those close to Wilson to conceal news of his serious condition are well-known. His case was not unique. One of FDR's secretaries, Jonathan Daniels, wrote: "..it was my job to screen all the grisly pictures of FDR which had been flown back from Yalta and to release only those which seemed least marked by what afterward we understood was his dying" [49].

White House physicians in the past have been less than truthful in their public statements on their patients' health [8]. Drs. Grayson (for Wilson), McIntire (for FDR), Travell (for Kennedy), and Burkley (for Johnson) gave misleading information and cooperated with efforts to hide the truth of their patients' medical conditions.

142

If it is true that American presidents and Soviet leaders — as well as those of other countries — are commonly affected by illness, and if the impact of disease on the cognitive processes is as profound as it has been shown to be, then the mechanisms for removing temporarily disabled heads of state from their primary decision-making role in time of crisis must be carefully crafted and utilized whenever necessary. But even when the procedures are in place, their implementation may be resisted or avoided.

A contemporary example was the demand on President Reagan in March, 1981 that he continue to function in his presidential role following the assassination attempt by John Hinkley. The aftermath of trauma, blood loss, a collapsed lung, surgery, anesthesia, and infection placed a large burden on a disabled individual. This took place at a time when internal unrest in Poland was so intense that the Administration spokesmen repeatedly expressed the conviction that a Soviet invasion of Poland was imminent.

Nevertheless, while the Constitutional mechanism for temporary replacement was at hand, it was not utilized for several reasons. A major factor was the confusion in the President's entourage between biologic survival, on the one hand, and the preservation by the President of his full cognitive capacities for decision making in crisis, on the other.

These issues may have been of lesser importance in another age, when transportation and communication placed limited demands for rapid responses to crisis and when our great technological skills had not yet provided the capacity for annihilation of much of the globe. They cannot be avoided or deferred in the modern era.

Contingency systems function only as well as the persons charged with making them work. In the Reagan episode, the Constitutional mechanisms for temporary succession did not fail, but the authorities did. A first priority for a new administration — in the United States, the Soviet Union, or in any country — must be the assurance that the plans for succession are ready for implementation if required. Rehearsal of crisis and succession procedures should occur from the first day of the transition, and regularly thereafter. The collective memory should be passed on as *the emergency books* — not even available in the White House on March 30, 1981 — from each administration to the next.

A mosaic of likely and unlikely scenarios should be constructed, indicating precisely when Section 3 or Section 4 of the 25th Amendment should be mandated, when used selectively, and when held in abeyance. More work is needed to define the mechanism of invocation. Who will make the decision to use or not to use? Will it be the Vice-President and a majority of the Cabinet, as stipulated in the 25th Amendment? Or will it be the White House Chief of Staff, if he so chooses? What will be the role of physicians and psychiatrists in assessing the competence of the leader? How will we assure dispassionate appraisals?

Regardless of how these and corresponding questions are answered in different nations, a full public awareness of the condition of national leaders is an obligation that surely needs to be fulfilled. Monitoring their health and well-being is important to everyone's health and well-being. In the United States, we have a lower limit on the age of candidates for a presidency; we might well consider an upper limit.

After all, Roosevelt was 63 when he died and was in chronic heart failure when he ran for a fourth term as President of the United States. Eisenhower was 62 when he became President and then had a heart attack in 1955, regional enteritis, bowel obstruction, and surgery in 1956, and a stroke in 1957. President George Bush is now 65, an age in which the incidence of heart attacks, strokes and malignant neoplasms is appreciable. Beyond temporary replacement under the 25th Amendment, if history repeats itself and if the more than 20% of presidents who have died in office or been impeached are a fair sample, Vice President Dan Quayle has a better than 1 in 5 chance of becoming President Quayle within the next 4-8 years.

Which brings up one more important point: the next-in-line really does matter in the affairs of the great powers and the international community. It may be his/her decision in crisis and his/her finger on the button that we will all have to

144

rely on.

References

[1] George, Alexander "The Causal Nexus between Cognitive Beliefs and Decision-Making Behavior: The 'Operational Code' Belief System," in: **Psychological Models in International Politics** Falkowski, L. ed. (Boulder, CO: Westview Press, 1979)

[2] George, Alexander "The Impact of Crisis-Induced Stress on Decision Making," **The Medical Implications of Nuclear War** Institute of Medicine, National Academy of Science (Washington D.C.: National Academy Press, 1986), pp. 529-552

[3] Holsti, Ole "Crisis, Stress, and Decision Making," **International Social Science Journal**, Vol. 23, No. 1, 1971, pp. 53-67

[4] Milbourn, T. "The Management of Crises," in: **International Crises: Insights from Behavioral Research** Herman, C. ed. (New York: Free Press, 1972)

[5] Bronner, R. **Decision Making Under Time Pressure** (Lexington, MA: Lexington Books, 1982)

[6] Janis, Irving L. "Decisionmaking Under Stress" in: **Handbook of Stress: Theoretical and Clinical Aspects**, Leo Goldberger and Shlomo Breznitz, eds. (New York: The Free Press, 1982), pp. 69-87

[7] Dixon, Norman. "The Illusion of Rational Decision Making" Presentation at the Workshop on Accidental Nuclear War, Third Annual Congress, International Physicians for the Prevention of Nuclear War, Amsterdam, June 17-22, 1983

[8] Abrams, Herbert L. "Inescapable Risk: Human Disability and 'Accidental' Nuclear War" **Current Research on Peace and Violence** Vol. XI, Nos. 1-2, 1988

[9] Cay, Elisabeth L., Vetter, N., Philip, A. E. and Dugard, Pat "Psychological Status During Recovery from an Acute Heart Attack" **Journal of Psychosomatic Research**, vol. 16, 1972, pp. 425-435

[10] Cay, Elisabeth L., Vetter, N., Philip, A. E. and Dugard, Pat "Psychological Reactions to a Coronary Care Unit" **Journal of Psychosomatic Research,** Vol. 16, 1972,

pp. 437-447

[11] Cay, Elisabeth L., Vetter, N., Philip, A. E. and Dugard, Pat "Return to Work after a Heart Attack" **Journal of Psychosomatic Research,** Vol. 17, 1973, pp. 231-243

[12] Doehrman, Steven R. "Psycho-Social Aspects of Recovery from Coronary Heart Disease: A Review." **Social Science and Medicine,** Vol. 11, 1977, pp. 199-218

[13] Kavanagh, T., Shephard, R.J., and Tuck, J.A. "Depression After Myocardial Infarction." **Canadian Medical Association Journal,** Vol. 113, 1975, pp. 23-27

[14] Leegaard, Ole F. "Diffuse Cerebral Symptoms in Convalescents from Cerebral Infarction and Myocardial Infarction" **Acta Neurologica Scandinavica** Vol. 67, 1983, pp. 348-355.

[15] Hertzog, Christopher, Schaie, K. Warner and Gribbin, Kathy "Cardiovascular Disease and Changes in Intellectual Functioning from Middle to Old Age" **Journal of Gerontology** Vol. 33, No. 6, 1978, pp. 872-883

[16] Eisdorfer, Carl and Wilkie, Frances. "Stress, Disease, Aging and Behavior" in: **Handbook of the Psychology of Aging.** (New York: Van Nostrand Reinhold Company, 1977), pp. 251-275

[17] Storey, P.B. "Brain Damage and Personality Change after Subarachnoid Haemorrhage" **British Journal of Psychiatry,** Vol. 117, 1970, pp. 129-142

[18] Short, M.J., Wilson, W.P. and Odom, G.L. "Psychiatric Sequelae of Subarachnoid Hemorrhage" **Southern Medical Journal,** Vol. 61, Jan. 1968, pp. 87-91

[19] Ebrahim, Shah, Nouri, Fiona and Barer, David. "Cognitive Impairment After Stroke" **Age and Ageing,** Vol. 14, 1985, pp. 345-350

[20] Folstein, Marshal F., Maiberger, Richard and McHugh, Paul R. "Mood Disorder as a Specific Complication of Stroke" **Journal of Neurology, Neurosurgery, and Psychiatry,** Vol. 40, 1977, pp. 1018-1020

[21] Levine, David N. and Finklestein, Seth. "Delayed Psychosis After Right Temporoparietal Stroke or Trauma: Relation to Epilepsy" **Neurology,** Vol. 32,

Mar. 1982, pp. 267-273

[22] Lishman, William A. **Organic Psychiatry, the Psychological Consequences of Cerebral Disorder** (Palo Alto: Blackwell Scientific Publications, 1987)

[23] Andreasen, Nancy C. "Posttraumatic Stress Disorder" in: Kaplan, Friedman, Sadock. **Comprehensive Textbook of Psychiatry**, Vol. III, (New York: Williams and Wilkins, 1980), pp. 1517-1525

[24] Titchener, James L. "Management and Study of Psychological Response to Trauma" **Journal of Trauma**, vol. 10, No. 11, 1970, pp. 974-980

[25] Lenehan, Gail Pisarcik. "Emotional Impact of Trauma" **Nursing Clinics of North America**, Vol. 21, No. 4, 1981, pp. 517-525

[26] Mesulam, Marek-Marsel and Geschwind, Norman. "Disordered Mental States in the Postoperative Period" **Urologic Clinics of North America**, Vol. 3, No. 2, June 1976, pp. 199-215

[27] Green, Stephen A. **Mind and Body: The Psychology of Physical Illness** (Washington D.C.: American Psychiatric Press, Inc., 1985)

[28] Surman, Owen S. "The Surgical Patient" in: **Massachusetts General Hospital Handbook of General Hospital Psychiatry**, Thomas P. Hackett and Ned H. Cassem, eds. (St. Louis: The C.V. Mosby Company, 1978), pp. 65-92

[29] Hsu, Jing. "Depression in Cancer Patients: An Overview" **Hawaii Medical Journal**, Vol. 45, No. 8, Aug. 1986, pp. 272-290

[30] Maguire, Peter. "The Psychological Impact of Cancer" **British Journal of Hospital Medicine**, Vol. 34, No. 2, Aug.1985, pp. 100-103

[31] Morris, Carol A. "Self-Concept as Altered by the Diagnosis of Cancer" **Nursing Clinics of North America**, Vol. 20, No.4, Dec. 1985, pp. 611-630

[32] Lloyd, G.G, Parker, A.C. and Ludlam, C.A. "Emotional Impact of Diagnosis and Early Treatment of Lymphomas" **Journal of Psychosomatic Research**, Vol. 28, No. 2, 1984, pp. 157-162

[33] Silberfarb, Peter M. "Chemotherapy and Cognitive

Defects in Cancer Patients" **Annual Review of Medicine**, Vol. 34, 1983, pp. 35-46

[34] Apter, Nathaniel S., Halstead, Ward C. and Heimburger, Robert F. "Cerebral Complications in Essential Hypertension" **Transcripts of the American Neurological Association**, 1949, pp. 219-222

[35] Francheschi, Massimo, Tancredi, Olga, Smirne, Salvatore, Mercinelli, Anna and Canal, Nicola. "Cognitive Processes in Hypertension" **Hypertension**, Vol. 4, No. 2, Mar-Apr. 1982, pp. 226-229.

[36] Spieth, Walter. "Cardiovascular Health Status, Age, and Psychological Performance" **Journal of Gerontology**, Vol. 19, 1964, pp. 277-284.

[37] Eisdorfer, "Stress, Disease, Aging and Behavior"

[38] Vaernes, Ragnar J., Owe, Jan 0. and Myking, Ole. "Central Nervous Reactions to ta 6.5-Hour Altitude Exposure at 3048 Meters" **Aviation, Space, and Environmental Medicine**, Vol. 55, Oct. 1984, pp. 921-926

[39] Kelman, G.R. and Crow, T.J. "Impairment of Mental Performance at a Simulated Altitude of 8,000 Feet" **Aerospace Medicine**, Vol. 40, No. 9, 1969, pp. 981-982

[40] Leavitt, Fred **Drugs and Behavior** (New York: John Wiley and Sons, Inc., 1982)

[41] Korttila, Kari, Linnoila, Markku, Ertama, Pertti, and Hakkinen, Sauli "Recovery and Simulated Driving After Intravenous Anesthesia with Thiopental, Methohexithal, Propanidid, or Alphadione" **Anesthesiology**, Vol. 43, No. 3, Sept. 1975, pp. 291-299

[42] Trounce, J.R. **Clinical Pharmacology for Nurses** (New York: Churchill Livingstone, 1985)

[43] Mandler, George "Stress and Thought Process" in: **Handbook of Stress: Theoretical and Clinical Aspects** Leo Goldberger and Shlomo Breznitz, eds. (New York: The Free Press, 1982), pp. 88-104

[44] Swanson, David W. "Clinical Psychiatric Problems Associated with General Surgery" in: **Psychological Aspects of Surgery, International Psychiatry Clinics**, Abrams, H.S. ed., No. 4, (Boston: Little, Brown and Co, 1967), pp. 105-113

[45] Beck, Aaron T. **Depression: Clinical, Experimental and Theoretical Aspects** (New York: Harper and Row, 1967)

[46] Green, Stephen A. **Mind and Body: The Psychology of Physical Illness** (Washington D.C.: American Psychiatric Press, Inc., 1985)

[47] Weingartner, Herbert and Silberman, Edward. "Models of Cognitive Impairment: Cognitive Changes in Depression" **Psychopharmacology Bulletin**, Vol. 18, No. 2, Apr. 1982, pp. 27-42

[48] Scott, Diane W. "Anxiety, Critical Thinking and Information Processing During and After Breast Biopsy" **Nursing Research**, Vol. 32, No. 1, Jan. 1983, pp. 24-28

[49] Daniels, Jonathan. **The End of Innocence** (New York: J.B. Lippincott Company, 1954)

Psychiatry and Accidental Nuclear War: Is There a Connection?

Klaus Minde

Introduction

To prevent any war, negotiations between potential adversaries should be in the hands of people who are cool-headed and prone neither to anxiety, anger nor impulsive decisions. They should also value cooperation and be empathic with the thoughts and feelings of others.

There is good evidence that most adults with these characteristics have started out in life with a a secure attachment to their primary caretakers. In other words, early attachment is of the greatest importance in the development of a person. In the present paper I will therefore briefly describe how the level of emotional security or attachment experienced by a young child develops and becomes related to the child's later social competence, empathy and the degree of suspicion shown towards others. I will then make some suggestions about the possibilities to educate for peace and relate these suggestions to steps which may further the secure attachment of young children to those who care for them.

Psychological Factors of Accidental Nuclear War

The influence of the style of interpersonal behavior on the management of national and international crises has been studied by an increasingly sophisticated network of researchers. Beginning with the 1976 book by Robert Jervis, entitled **Perceptions and Misperceptions in International Politics** (Jervis, 1976), and followed by work from Cornell's Centre of Peace Studies (Jervis, Lebow and Stein, 1985, Lebow, 1987), as well as thoughtful appraisals by psychiatrists (e.g., Mack, 1984, 1986, 1988) and psychoanalysts (Meissner, 1988, Volkan 1988), there is now a good deal of information available about:

a) the circumstances which increase the likelihood of a

crisis and hence an accidental war; and

b) the psychological mechanisms which govern the decision-making capacities of leaders under stress.

Brecher (1978) states that the most pervasive factor that can create a crisis in the life of a nation is the perception by its leaders that there is a threat to the nation's survival or to the political philosophy of its government. This means that our sense of physical security and of what we are as individual members of a nation, which are both based on the same factors as our early personal attachments, must appear to be threatened by an outsider to create a perception of crisis. This perception is heightened by a significant component of uncertainty about the enemy often present in such situations. Thus, the challenged group or their leader(s) often know little about detailed plans of the adversary and therefore assume a *worst possible scenario*. A leader facing an outside attack also generally fears that this disunity within his or her own group will increase unless some almost magic decisive action is taken by him or her. This increases the sense of urgency which invariably accompanies a crisis. In fact, there is now general consensus among social scientists that the most central threat to any positive crisis resolution (in our context especially a crisis involving a potential nuclear attack) is related to the brief time span given a leader to decide on the action to be taken. As the protagonists are usually aware of the gravity and importance of their decision and want to act responsibly, they initially try to absorb an ever increasing amount of information about the crisis at hand. This generally leads to an over-loading of their cognitive system which results in a switch from reason to emotion. While this switch will decrease the sense of anxiety and pressure, it also leads to a cessation of communication between the involved adversarial groups and the development of a specific defensive position, which has been called "defensive avoidance" (Jervis et al, 1986). This avoidance response is characterized by a) procrastination, i.e., an attempt to avoid a decision which cannot deal with all the important variables of the crisis and; b) shifting the responsibility for the decision to someone else; and c) *bolstering*. This last strategy is possibly the most dangerous one to respond to a threat. It consists of presenting the least objectionable among many unsatisfactory choices as positive, thereby often extinguishing the wish to look for other alternatives. It also makes negotiations between adversaries less likely and increases the projection of *bad qualities* into others.

Bolstering has been used in such clearly disastrous and unnecessary confrontations as the Falkland crisis of 1982 (Lebow, 1987), the SDI debate, and the ongoing confrontations in the Middle East.

Defensive avoidance is also associated with a lack of empathy for the adversary since the perception of the other as implacably hostile works against the ability to take the perspective of the other party and to assess the constraints and pressures the other may also be subjected to. Nisbett and Ross (1980) have furthermore documented that politicians under stress often make a fundamental attribution error because they see the actions of others as an expression of basic predispositions or characterological givens (e.g., Russia wants to take over the world) while their own actions are understood to be a response to *situational pressures* (e.g., America has to defend itself). Such motivational biases are very difficult to overcome as they are often sanctioned by a vociferous part of the population and appear to offer easier decision making procedures. In fact, Nisbett and Ross (1980) as well as Lebow (1987) have concluded that the stress experienced by potential decision makers over war and peace is so intense that these individuals often develop acute dissociative states during which they become quite indecisive and are easily influenced by others. For example, there is historical evidence both Kaiser Wilhelm I, following the declaration of World War I, and Stalin, following the German invasion of the Soviet Union in 1941, experienced dissociative states which lasted for up to 3 days (Zhukov, 1971, Lebow, 1981).

Psychoanalytic thinkers such as Meissner (1988) believe that the unbearable stress associated with any severe crisis heightens helplessness and vulnerabilities in an individual leader. This reawakens old memories of traumatic episodes and brings back the possible failures of early caretakers in comforting and soothing the leader as a child. In other words, individuals in leadership positions who experienced an insecure attachment towards their early caretakers will be more likely to develop a *sense of victim* which helps them to rationalize their own aggressive actions and can lead to an increasingly paranoid state of mind.

Early Attachment and its Relevance
for Later Psychosocial Functioning

Some fifty years ago a group of physicians demonstrated the pervasive ill effects of institutional and hospital care on infants and young children (Goldfarb, 1943; Spitz, 1946). It appeared that children who had received outwardly adequate care during protracted hospitalizations or while living in *modern and hygienic* orphanages became increasingly sad and finally seemingly totally detached from their regular caregivers.

Significant numbers of these children also died without any apparent medical complications, to the puzzlement of the staff of these institutions.

These observations, together with specific ethological data, provided the theoretical underpinning of modern day attachment theory. This theory, developed primarily by Bowlby and described by him in three volumes, entitled Attachment (1969), Separation (1973) and Loss (1980), understands attachment to be a *system* composed of attachment behaviors that operate to keep the infant and mother in close proximity. The term *system* is used in the sense of a control system in engineering. Bowlby states that young infants in early history needed to be physically close to their mothers to be protected against potential outside dangers. This previously biological necessity has, according to him, now become instinctive in a ethological sense, i.e., it is necessary for normal development of any human being to take place. Attachment, then, is a biological construct which shows itself in the desire of the infant to be in proximity to its caretaker. This desire is expressed from approximately two months onward by different behaviors such as a preferential smiling and reaching for the caretaker, frequent visual checks on the parent (also called referencing) and the obvious preference in affection shown to parents over other adults. If the attachment system works smoothly the baby will show little anxiety during his day to day activities and other parameters, such as his wish to explore the world, can develop freely. In other words, babies who are securely attached can expend their energies exploring the world around them rather than worrying about their mothers and their own place in the world.

How do these early attachment experiences relate to a child's later life? Bowlby (1980) states that through transactions with the world of persons and objects, children construct increasingly complex "internal working models" of our world and of the significant persons in it (Bowlby, 1980). These models serve to assess and guide behavior in new situations. For example, if the child's experience has led him or her to construct a model of the mother (or other attachment figure) as likely to provide support when needed, close monitoring of her whereabouts may be less necessary than when such responsiveness cannot be counted on. On the other hand, an infant who has learned that his mother tends to dismiss his attempts to gain comfort from her when in distress will need to spend far more energy to keep track of her whereabouts so as not to lose her altogether. However, as the individual matures and in order to remain in touch with the real world, internal working models of attachment figures, social partners and the physical world must be readjusted to meet changing realities. Thus, as children become better able to assess the intentions and motives of their caretakers, as they acquire improved coping skills and learn to make better appraisals of what is dangerous, attachment behavior becomes more subtle. In older children and adults the power of the attachment system expresses itself therefore overtly only in stressful situations. This is not, however, a sign that the attachment system becomes less important.

We need to recognize that the attachment system reflects on our feelings about the world outside as well as our view of ourselves. For example, if a mother frequently rejects or ridicules the child's requests for comfort in stressful situations, the child may come to develop not only an internal working model of the parent as rejecting but also one of himself or herself as not worthy of help and comfort. This means that a child who trusts his parents to give needed emotional support will also learn the complimentary parental role, that is, how to be empathic and, later on, how to be a sensitive parent or partner.

How can we evaluate the quality of attachment an infant has toward his or her caretaker? Some ten years ago Mary Ainsworth (Ainsworth et al, 1978) published a study where she reported on a method of assessing attachment by exposing twelve to eighteen month-old infants to a series of increasingly stressful episodes. On the basis of how the baby copes with these stressors, Ainsworth characterized the infant's quality of attachment into three reliable classifications: secure, avoidant and resistant. Secure infants approached the mother upon her return and sought physical contact with her if they had been overtly distressed by the separation experience. If they had not become distressed, they greeted her and sought interaction from her. Avoidant children snubbed or avoided the mother on her return, while the resistant group showed angry, resistant behavior interspersed with attachment behavior following the reunion with their mothers.

Findings from different investigations which used Ainsworth's paradigm have shown that, among other things, the observed behavior patterns at twelve and eighteen months predict a variety of emotional and behavioral characteristics of children at least up to the school years. For example, infants who were securely attached at twelve months have been shown to be more autonomous at age two (Matas et al, 1978), more socially competent with peers, and more self-reliant, flexible and involved in preschool and kindergarten (Arend et al,1979). The observed quality of attachment also functions as a predictor of behavior problems at five years. Erickson et al (1985) and Main et al (1985) found long term continuities of secure or insecure social behaviors to extend well into late primary school age.

While these findings cannot be automatically extended to embrace adult behavior, the likelihood is very strong that attachment patterns and the ensuing working models have a powerful influence on the type of communication, problem solving, and mutuality a person uses in later life. Thus our internal working models contain within them our basic assessment of the world we live in, which, in turn, determines our relationships with others and our sense about ourselves.

It should be stressed that the soundness of our early attachment relationships does not alone determine the later leadership qualities of a person. Individuals are born with many diverse characteristics such as certain temperamental dispositions and varying intellectual abilities. These characteristics will be more or less helpful when assuming leadership roles. Attachments and consequently our thoughts about the world also change in later life in response to specific experiences. Nevertheless, the relevance of the construct of attachment in assessing our leaders appears to be secured although little work has been done in this area in the past.

The Possibilities for Education for Peace

As our discussion shows, the foundations of the institution of war are made up not only by specific economic, religious or historical factors, but also by such human factors as interpersonal distrust of individual leaders or groups and lack of empathy and perspective taking. We have also seen the importance such issues as the fear of the unknown (or of what is strange) have in the institution of war (Hinde and Bateson, 1989). While any change in the complex psychosocial functioning of an individual or a group is difficult to obtain, the social sciences have provided us with sufficient data to suggest how the fear of the unknown can be reduced and the level of empathy and perspective taking raised in an individual.

The first and foremost task is to increase the general awareness of professionals to the importance of furthering secure attachment relationships between parents and their young children. This can be done in a variety of ways through education and modelling. Detailed descriptions can be found in the work of Fraiberg (1959), Minde (1986) and Provence & Naylor (1983).

In addition to practicing prevention by sensitizing caretakers to the emotional needs of young children, the following steps should be considered in the endeavour to eliminate the crucial elements of human psychology from among the reasons for an accidental nuclear war:

1. We must become more aware of our rationalizations. As was stated previously, leaders facing an international crisis often develop a stance of *defensive avoidance*. This makes them get stuck on one particular management technique and compromises their ability to see other available options. In addition, leaders also have been shown to think they can manage a crisis by manipulating the degree of military or political escalation (Lebow, 1987). This has always led to failure. On the other hand, the recent peaceful uprisings of large segments of nations in Eastern Europe have shown the power of non-violent protest against entrenched systems whose validation used to come from national leaders.**

2. We can minimize the probability of an escalation of tension by creating personal bonds between adversaries. This can be done by increasing opportunities for interpersonal exchange between students and professionals with countries in opposing camps. Stephenson (1984) has shown that such exchanges make it hard for the stronger party to exploit the weaker group later on.

3. We may be able to engage present day and potential future leaders in exercises of emotional role playing as developed by Nisbett and Ross (1980). Such exercises, which can also be part of the general school curriculum (UNESCO 1983) do all of the following:

*** Editor's Note: This revised text was received in December, 1989.*

a) they highlight the interdependence of all inhabitants of this planet, especially in relation to the world's ecology, trade links and cultural diversity. This means they further the notion that there are not simply good and bad but many differing value systems which all try to cope with the global issues confronting this world;

b) they assist people to recognize differences in the functioning of individuals and groups. This is especially important since opinion formation and decision-making by individuals and those deciding as members of groups are quite different (Fraser and Foster, 1984). Thus group members usually define themselves by their group and not by their independent selves. They also follow specific rules and regulations made by the group. In contrast to individuals, however, the cohesion within groups is not based on personal relationships but on a specific identity such as *the soldier* or *the nation* (Rabbie and Horwitz, 1969). This can make for a more distorted vision of reality;

c) they foster the learning of empathy and prosocial behavior. As the degree of empathy a person possesses is clearly related to his early experiences with his or her major attachment figures (Radke-Yarrow et al. 1983), early intervention here promises to be most effective. Feshbach and her colleagues, in fact, have developed a curriculum for school-age children which has been successful in teaching empathy and in leading to a decrease in overall aggressive behavior (Feshbach, 1989). Similar exercises are available to assist adolescents and older individuals to take the perspective of potential adversaries and assume their role in an enactment of specific conflict situations. This approach seems especially promising in view of the continuities of prosocial behavior between childhood and adulthood, as traced by Lieven (1989).

Furthermore, since empathic responding tends to foster feelings of attachment towards the empathic individual, such programs may indeed lead to less stereotyped political responses towards those holding different political and ideological convictions.

Conclusion

The present paper has attempted to touch on some psychological phenomena which are related to the basis of war and has outlined some measures which may assist in the struggle against the institution of war.

It also documents that early relationships may be an important determinant of an individual's later leadership style.

Acknowledgement

This paper benefited from the help and encouragement received from John Bowlby and Robert Hinde. Both read an earlier version and made important and helpful comments.

Notes

Ainsworth, M.D.S., Blehar, M.C., Waters, E., and Wall, S., **Patterns of Attachment: A Psychological Study of the Strange Situation** (Hillsdale, N.J.: Erlbaum, 1978)

Arend, R., Gove, F., Sroufe, L.A., "Continuity of individual adaptation from infancy to kindergarten: A predictive study of ego-resiliency and curiosity in preschoolers" **Child Development**, Vol. 50, pp. 950-959, 1979

Bowlby, J., **Attachment and Loss: Vol. 1. Attachment** (New York: Basic Books, 1969)

Bowlby, J., **Attachment and Loss: Vol. 2. Separation** (New York: Basic Books, 1973)

Bowlby, J., **Attachment and Loss: Vol. 3. Loss, Sadness, and Depression.** (New York: Basic Books, 1980)

Bowlby, J., **Attachment and Loss: Vol. 1. Attachment (2d)** (New York: Basic Books, 1982)

Erickson, M.F., Sroufe, L.A., and Egeland, B. "The relationship of quality of attachment and behavior problems in preschool in a high risk sample" In: **Growing points of attachment theory and research**, I. Bretherton and E. Waters, eds. Monographs of the Society for Research in Child Development, Vol. 50 (1-2, Serial No. 209), (1985) pp. 147-186

Feshbach, N.D., "Empathy training and prosocial behavior" In: **Aggression and War** J. Groebel & R.H. Hinde, eds. (1989) pp. 101-111

Fraiberg, S., **The Magic Years: Understanding and Handling the Problems of Early Childhood** (New York: Scribner, 1959)

Fraser, C., Foster, D., "Social groups, nonsense groups and group polarization" In: **The Social Dimension** Vol. 2. H. Tajfel, ed. (Cambridge: Cambridge University Press, 1984) pp. 473-497

Goldfarb, W., "Infant rearing and problem behavior" **American Journal of Orthopsychiatry** Vol. 13, (1943) pp. 249-256

Hinde, R.A., Bateson, P., "Some goals in education for peace" In: **Education for Peace** R.A. Hinde & P.H. Perry, eds. (Nottingham: Russell Press, 1989) pp 10-17

Jervis, R., **Perception and Misperception in International Politics** (Princeton, N.J.: Princeton University Press, 1976)

Jervis, R., Lebow, R.N., and Stein, J.G., **Psychology and Deterrence** (Baltimore, Maryland: Johns Hopkins University Press, 1985)

Lebow, R.N. , **Between Peace and War. The Nature of International Crisis** (Baltimore: Johns Hopkins University Press, 1981) pp 135-145

Lebow, R.N., **Nuclear Crisis Management: A Dangerous Illusion** (Ithaca, NY: Cornell University Press, 1987)

Lieven, E., "The psychological basis of cooperation and caring" In: **Education for Peace.** R.A. Hinde & Y.H. Perry, eds. (Nottingham: Russell Press, 1989) pp 79-87

Mack, J.E., "Resistances to knowing in the nuclear age" **Harvard Educational Review** (1984) Vol. 54, pp. 260-270

Mack, J.E., "Nuclear weapons and the dark side of human kind" **Political Psychology** (1986) Vol. 7, pp. 223-233

Mack, J.E, "The enemy system" **The Lancet** August, 1988, pp 385-387

Main, M., Kaplan, N. and Cassidy, J., "Security in infancy, childhood and adulthood: A move to the level of representation" In: **Growing points of attachment theory and research**, I. Bretherton and E. Waters, eds. Monographs of the Society for the Research in Child Development Vol. 50 (1-2, Serial 209, 1985)

Main, M. and Cassidy, J., "Categories of response to reunion with the parent at age 6: Predictable from infant attachment classifications and stable over a 1-month period" **Developmental Psychology** Vol. 24 (1988) pp. 415-426

Matas, L., Arend, R.A., and Stroufe, L.A., "Continuity of adaptation in the second year: The relationship between quality of attachment and later competence" **Child Development** Vol. 49 (1978) pp. 547-556

Meissner, W.W., "Impending nuclear disaster" In: **Psychoanalysis and the Nuclear Threat** H.B.Levine, D. Jacobs, and L.J. Rubin, eds. (Hillsdale, N.J.: The Analytic Press, 1988) pp 111-129

Minde, K., "Bonding and attachment: Its relevance for the present day clinician" **Developmental Medicine Child Neurology** Vol. 28 (1986) pp. 803-813

Nisbett, R. and Ross, L., **Human Inference: Strategies and Shortcomings of Social Judgement** (Englewood, N.J.: Prentice Hall, 1980) pp. 120-138 and 273-295

Provence, S., Naylor, A., **Working with Disadvantaged Parents and their Children** (New Haven, Ct: Yale University Press, 1983)

Rabbie, J.M., Horwitz, M. , "The arousal of ingroup and outgroup bias by a chance to win or lose" **J. Pers. Soc. Psychol.** Vol. 69 (1969) pp. 223-228

Radke-Yarrow, M., Zahn-Waxler, C., Chapman, M., "Children's prosocial dispositions and behavior" In: **Mussen Handbook of Child Psychology**, E.M. Hetherington (eds), Vol. 4 (New York: Wiley, 1983)

Spitz, R., "Anaclitic depression" **Psychoanalytic Study of the Child** Vol. 2, (1946) pp. 313-342

UNESCO, **Education for International Cooperation and Peace at the Primary School Level**, (Paris: Unesco, 1983)

Volkan, V.D., "Nuclear weapons and the need to have enemies. A psychoanalytic perspective" In:

Psychoanalysis and the Nuclear Threat H.B. Levine, D. Jacobs, L.J. Rubin, eds. (Hillsdale, N.J.: The Analytic Press, 1988) pp 111-129

Zhukov, G., **The Memoirs of General Zhukov** (New York: Delacorte, 1971) pp. 234-236, 238

Workshop Participants

Authors of chapters in this book are indicated by asterisks **
and their biographies appear in the final section:
About the Authors.

Professor Herbert L. Abrams**
Professor Horst Afheldt **
Professor Ingemar Ahlstrand, State Office for Financial
Control, Stockholm, Sweden
Professor Viola W. Bernard, Department of Psychiatry,
College of Physicians and Surgeons, Columbia University,
New York, USA
Mr Derek Boothby, Principal Officer, Department for
Disarmament Affairs, United Nations, New York, USA
Dr Morris Bradley**
Dr Giovanni Brenciaglia, Nuclear Fuel Physics and Heavy
Water Inc., Toronto; Chairman, Pugwash Park
Commission, Pugwash, Canada
Professor Shlomo Breznitz, Professor of Psychology,
Director, R. D. Wolfe Centre for Study of Psychological
Stress, University of Haifa, Haifa, Israel
Mr Maxwell Bruce, Queen's Counsel, London, UK; Secretary,
British Pugwash Group
Professor Francesco Calogero, Professor of Theoretical
Physics, University of Rome "La Sapienza", Rome, Italy;
Secretary-General, Pugwash Conferences on Science and
World Affairs
Mrs Anne Eaton, Pugwash Park Commission, Pugwash, Nova
Scotia, Canada
Professor Alexander L. George**
Academician Vitalii Goldanskii, Director, Institute of
Chemical Physics, Academy of Sciences, Moscow, USSR;
Member of Executive Committee of Pugwash Conferences
on Science and World Affairs
Professor Kurt Gottfried**
Professor John P. Holdren, Professor of Energy and
Resources, University of California, Berkeley, CA, USA;
Chairman of the Executive Committee of Pugwash
Conferences on Science and World Affairs
Professor Michael D. Intriligator**

163

Dr Martin M. Kaplan, Consultant, World Health Organisation, Geneva, Switzerland; former Secretary-General, Pugwash Conferences on Science and World Affairs

Professor Vitalii Kuleshov, Deputy Head, Physics and Mathematics Section, Academy of Sciences, Moscow, USSR

Lt-General (ret.) Lloyd R. Leavitt, Jr., (USAF), President Qualitech, Palos Verdes, CA, USSR

General Mikhail Milstein, Consultant to Institute for USA and Canada Studies, Academy of Sciences, Moscow, USSR

Professor Klaus Minde**

Professor Maciej Nalecz, Director, Institute of Biocybernetics and Biomedical Engineering, Warsaw, Poland; Chairman, Council of Pugwash Conferences on Science and World Affairs

Professor Oleg Olkhov, Institute of Chemical Physics, Academy of Sciences, Moscow, USSR

Professor Derek Paul**

Professor Rita Rogers**

Professor Joseph Rotblat, Emeritus Professor of Physics, University of London, UK; President, Pugwash Conferences on Science and World Affairs

Dr Victor M. Sergeev, Institute for USA and Canada Studies, Academy of Sciences, Moscow, USSR

Dr Paul Smoker**

Mr Ray Szabo, Pugwash Park Commission, Pugwash, Nova Scotia, Canada. CSX Corporation, Richmond, VA, USA

Professor Michael D. Wallace**

About the Authors

Herbert L. Abrams is an international authority on cardiovascular radiology. He is Professor of Radiology at Stanford University School of Medicine and a Member-in-Residence of the Stanford University Center for International Security and Arms Control. As National Co-Chairman of Physicians for Social Responsibility, and as Founding Vice President of International Physicians for the Prevention of Nuclear War — winner of the 1985 Nobel Peace Award — he has had the opportunity to increase the awareness of his colleagues, the public and policy makers as to the medical implications of nuclear weapons and nuclear war.

Horst Afheldt served in the German Armed Forces from 1943-1945. He studied Physics and Law in Strasbourg and Hamburg. He was General Manager of the Federation of German Scientists, from 1961 to 1971; and fellow at the Max-Planck-Institute on the Preconditions of Human Life in the Modern World in Starnberg from 1970-1981. Until his recent retirement he was Director of the Working Group Afheldt in the Max-Planck-Society. His most recent publications include: *Atomkrieg. Das Verhängnis einer Politik mit militärischne Mitteln (The Doom of Power Politics with Nuclear Means* (Munich: Hanser Publ., 1984)) and *Pour une Défense Non Suicidaire en Europe* (Paris: Editions La Découverte).

Morris Bradley received his Doctorate in Psychology from Birkbeck College, London University. He lectures at Strathclyde University, Glasgow in biological psychology. He is Co-Director of the Richardson Institute for Peace Studies at Lancaster University. For several years the Richardson Institute has been a focus of international initiatives to promote research into the risks of accidents with nuclear weapons, including accidental nuclear war. His research includes the study of beliefs about human nature and the value systems that underlie our complex and often ambiguous attitudes toward cooperation and competition, peace and security.

165

Dagobert L. Brito is the Peterkin Professor of Political Economy at Rice University. He has taught at the University of Wisconsin, Madison; at Ohio State University, where he was a Professor of Economics and of Political Science and Fellow of the Mershon Center; and at Tulane University where he was Director of the Murphy Institute for Political Economy. His research interests include arms races and war, topics in public economies, and economic theory. He is coeditor, with Michael D. Intriligator and Adele E. Wick, of *Strategies for Managing Nuclear Proliferation*, (Lexington Books, 1983) and coauthor, with Michael D. Intriligator, of *Arms Control: Problems and Prospects* (University of California Institute on Global Conflict and Cooperation, 1987).

Alexander L. George is Graham H. Stuart Professor of International Relations at Stanford University. He received a PhD in political science from the University of Chicago. He is the author of many books including: *Deterrence in Foreign Policy* (with Richard Smoke, 1974), which won the 1975 Bancroft Prize; *The Limits of Coercive Diplomacy* (with David K. Hall and William E. Simons, 1971); *Presidential Decisionmaking in Foreign Policy* (1980); *Force and Statecraft* (with Gordon A. Craig, 1983); *Managing US-Soviet Rivalry* (1983) and *US-Soviet Cooperation* (with Philip J. Farley and Alexander Dallin, 1988). He is currently a member of the National Academy of Sciences Committee on Contributions of Behavioral and Social Science to the Prevention of Nuclear War.

Kurt Gottfried is a professor of physics at Cornell University. He was a co-founder of the Union of Concerned Scientists and serves on its Board of Directors. His publications relevant to the topic of this volume include articles on conventional arms control, antisatellite weapons and ballistic missile defense, and the study *Crisis Stability and Nuclear War* (Oxford, 1988) co-edited with Bruce G. Blair.

Michael D. Intriligator is Professor of Economics and Political Science, Director of the Center for International and Strategic Affairs, and Director of the Jacob Marschak Interdisciplinary Colloquium on Mathematics in the Behavioral Sciences at UCLA. His major research interests include mathematical economic theory and econometrics and their applications to health economics and strategy and arms control and he has published four books in these areas. He has also edited and co-edited a number of books including: *National Security and International Stability* (with Bernard Brodie and Roman Kolkowicz, 1983), *Strategies for Managing Nuclear Proliferation* (with Dagobert L. Brito and Adele E. Wick, 1983) and *East-West Conflict: Elite Perceptions and Political Options* (with Hans-Adolf Jacobsen, 1988).

Klaus Minde, MD, is Professor of Psychiatry and Pediatrics at McGill University. He received his medical school training in Munich, and London, England, and was trained in psychiatry, psychology, pediatrics and psychoanalysis at McGill and Columbia Universities. He has worked as a child psychiatrist and researcher at McGill and the University of Toronto and served as a consultant for the World Health Organization in Uganda. More recently, until 1989, he was Chairman of Psychiatry at Queen's University.

Derek Paul is a professor of physics at the University of Toronto, in the fields of atomic and nuclear physics. He became a Pugwash participant in 1976. In 1981 he helped to found Science for Peace, a Canadian charitable corporation, and was its first treasurer/vice-president. He has held various offices in Science for Peace and is now Publications Director. In 1985 he organized a conference on European Security and edited the proceedings "Defending Europe: Options for Security" (Taylor and Francis, 1986), and has edited a book series "The Canadian Papers in Peace Studies", which began in 1988. He is currently a member of the "Consultative Group on Arms Control and Disarmament" of the Canadian Ambassador for Disarmament.

Ib Damgaard Petersen is an international relations scholar at the Institute of Political Studies, University of Copenhagen. He graduated as an historian and later specialized in international relations with emphasis on the study of international conflict. Active in the study of international conflict since the sixties, he has developed a unique methodology for the study of processes of conflict based on stochastic models. He has published two books on his methodology as well as books on the dynamics of the international system and on the Danish resistance movement.

Rita R. Rogers, MD, is a clinical professor of Psychiatry at UCLA. She is a graduate of the Vienna University Medical School and has a Masters in International Relations. She was trustee at large of the American Psychiatric Association from 1979-81 and chaired task forces on Pakistani-Bangladesh, Cyprus, and Arab-Israeli conflicts. She is the author of 85 publications in professional journals about psychiatry and foreign affairs and co-author of *The Alchemy of Survival* (Addison Welsley Publishing).

Paul Smoker is Co-Director of the Richardson Institute for Peace Studies, Lancaster University and Visiting Professor of International Peace Studies at Ritsumeikan University, Kyoto. He has worked in peace research since 1960 and his published more than 60 books, monographs, and academic papers in the field. He has recently published a monograph with Ib D. Petersen on the relationship between international tension and the probability of accidental nuclear war. He edits *International Peace Research Newsletter* for the International Peace Research Association.

Michael D. Wallace is Professor of Political Science at the University of British Columbia. He received his degrees at McGill and the University of Michigan. He is Vice-President of the United Nations Association in Canada and President of the British Columbia Chapter of Science for Peace. In 1982 he received the Karl W. Deutsch Peace Research Award. In 1986 he organized a conference in Vancouver, sponsored by Science for Peace, on Accidental Nuclear War.

SLCM — Submarine-launched cruise missiles
SLOC — sea lanes of communication
SSBN — Ballistic missile submarine
SSN — attack submarine
START — strategic arms reduction talks
TAC — Threat assessment conference
TEC — Threat evaluation conference
TOW — tube-launched, optically tracked, wire-guided
      (missile)
WINTEX — NATO's winter military exercise in Europe
WEIS — World Event Interaction Study
WTO — Warsaw Treaty Organisation (the Warsaw Pact)